Last Isle Stole!

Who Really Owns Last Island?
The 165-Year-long Battle for an Island…and the Truth

To Nicole,
Best Wishes
Jeanette Vavein

This Book is dedicated to

James Voisin Sr December 18, 1944 – January 8, 2009 the Alpha.

William Dixon June 7, 1943 – April 13, 2015 the Omega

and all the people that believed

Table of Contents

Prologue

Chapter One: *"To Jean Voisin, a Small Island…"*

Chapter Two: Louisiana, a State of Transition

Chapter Three: *"Now you see it…Now you don't!"*

Chapter Four: Opening Salvos

Chapter Five: Fishermen…

Chapter Six: …and Kings

Chapter Seven: August 1856 – A Great Storm, an Island Lost

Chapter Eight: A Slumbering Dispute Awakens

Chapter Nine: Had the BLM Found its *"Honest Man?"*

Chapter Ten: History's Search for True North

Chapter Eleven: For the BLM – Was the Past Prologue or Pretext?

Chapter Twelve: The Subtle Seduction of Barataria Bay

Chapter Thirteen: Is a *"Small Island"* Really Small?

Chapter Fourteen: A Tale of Three Maps

Chapter Fifteen: Possession – Nine Points of the Law?

Chapter Sixteen: Resolution – Three Bites at the Apple

Chapter Seventeen: The Ever-shifting Face of Resolution

Chapter Eighteen: Lessons of the Labyrinth

Epilogue

Prologue

A thorn defends the rose, harming only those who would steal the blossom.

-     Chinese proverb

"Last Isle Stole from Voisin family."

The words scrawled on walls and sidewalks surrounding the Terrebonne Parish Courthouse in Houma, Louisiana, were crudely formed curiously puzzling - *"Last Isle Stole...."*

Someone stole *Isle Derniere* – Last Island ? Variations of the epithet appeared in at least sixteen different locations in and around the downtown area during the first week in January 2009. The cryptic messages prompted a flurry of questions. Why the sudden interest in Last Island? Why now? Who was left to even care? What was left of the island to even care about?

More than one hundred and fifty years have passed since the South's first great storm destroyed Last Island Village. In its wake, the hurricane left a ravaged, body-littered, debris-strewn barrier island. If a stunned south Louisiana citizenry chose to forget about the devastated island in its aftermath, Nature clearly had not. Four hundred Louisianans had gathered on the island that August day, just as they had been doing for the preceding nine years, intent only on swapping Louisiana's hot summer days for a brief respite, unfettered by worldly concerns and immersed in leisure.

By mid-afternoon on Sunday, August 10, 1856, powerful counter-clockwise winds and a massive nine-foot tidal surge passed directly over the island, decimating every structure on the island. The storm drowned or crushed an estimated two hundred men, women and children. The two hundred who survived were scattered indiscriminately about the devastated island or washed across Caillou Bay into Terrebonne Parish's harsh coastal marshlands.

To the south and east of the island, another one hundred and thirty perished as their vessels capsized in the roiling waters of the Gulf of Mexico. For survivors trapped on the debris-scattered island or strewn along a thirty-mile stretch of coastline, the desperate struggle to stay afloat and alive was just beginning. Their life and death struggle would last for weeks.

Occurring only four and one-half years before the outbreak of the Civil War, the trauma caused by the 1856 storm quickly gave way to more momentous concerns. Given the all-encompassing magnitude of events to come, memories of Last Island quickly faded from the State's collective consciousness.

The story of August 10, 1856, lay dormant for nearly thirty years. That, of course, changed in 1888, when renowned novelist Lafcadio Hearn resurrected the tragedy with publication of his masterpiece, *Chita: A Memory of Last Island.*

Those wistful antebellum days, like the Louisiana coastline itself, have given way to time. Thanks to seventeen decades of storms and erosion, the State's western-most barrier islands – once a single island twenty-two miles in length – are today little more than a rapidly shrinking archipelago comprised of four tiny spits of sand in the Gulf of Mexico – Raccoon, Whiskey, Trinity and East islands. Oceanographers and coastal geologists are of one mind with respect to Last Island's eventual fate. Time is rapidly running out. Soon, the remaining remnants of this once famous resort island, *Isles Dernieres*, will be no more.

And so, on a chilly January morning in 2009, the residents of Houma pondered those odd etchings and posed the obvious question. What was behind the rash of graffiti found on walls, sidewalks and curbs in and around the courthouse complex?

"Last Isle Stole...."

A few days after the defacing words first appeared, Houma *Courier* reporter Robert Zullo[1] offered a possible explanation.

"The message apparently refers to a dispute between descendants of the original owner of the Isles Dernieres – 'Last Islands' – an oil company and the federal and state government."

Zullo's article suggested that someone connected to a frustrated, long-suffering, Terrebonne Parish family was reacting to yet another loss in their long struggle to reclaim the island that their ancestors had once owned. To the members of the Voisin family, this latest loss was perhaps its most painful yet. It was an infinitely more personal loss.

On January 8, 2009, barely one week before the graffiti first appeared, sixty-four year-old James Voisin died of a heart attack. For nearly twenty years, Voisin had served as the family's voice in its costly, all-consuming struggle against government agencies and the legal system. Had his herculean efforts to reclaim title to Last Island exacted the ultimate toll? Zullo's story fueled such speculation.

One year earlier, almost to the month and day of James Voisin's death, the family began to sense that its long journey was likely to fall short of its destination. As so many governmental and legal entities had done before, the United States Federal Court of Appeals found an easy way out of the decades-long land dispute - the statute of limitations. It is a terminating strategy that few seasoned magistrates can resist and an option that Federal Court of Appeals Judge Lynn Bush eagerly seized.

In the matter of *James Voisin versus the United States of America*, the federal court judge was succinct and to the point.

"Defendant's motion to dismiss and memorandum in support thereof, filed on June 11, 2007, is GRANTED. The Clerk's Office is directed to ENTER final judgment in favor of defendant

---

[1] Houma *Courier* Robert Zullo elaborated on his theory in a January 19, 2009, article entitled *Graffiti Rooted in Centuries-old Land Dispute.*

DISMISSING plaintiff's complaint, without prejudice..."

"Each party shall bear its own costs."

The Voisins would bear their share of the court costs. Those cost, though, were far heavier than even Judge Lynne Bush could have contemplated. As had so often been the case, the judge may have found her way out of the controversy, but in doing so, merely set the stage for the beleaguered family to begin yet again.

Nature's continuing destruction of the barrier islands, civil war and its aftermath have served only to blur the State's memories of Last Island. More than one hundred and sixty years had passed when, on a January morning in 2009, residents of Houma paused, trying to make sense of the graffiti on the sidewalks and walls of the courthouse complex, trying to answer a single question.

Who really owned Last Island?

The family of James Voisin had their answer. It was an answer embedded in an old family story. It was a story that began long, long ago - October 30, 1788.

Chapter One: "To Jean Voisin, a Small Island..."

That was a land grant that came from King George and it had the "H" all over it. – Paul Hoffman

If Judge Lynn Bush's 2008 decision was short and succinct, so too were the descriptions in the hundreds of 18th century land grants issued by Spain's provisional governors in Louisiana. On October 30, 1788, Don Estevan Miro, Spanish Governor for Louisiana, issued one such grant, called an *Order of Survey*, to a thirty-eight year-old fisherman and farmer from France, Jean Voisin.

"A Juan Voisin, una pequeña ysla, vulgarmente llamada L'Isle Longue, situado en el Lago de Barrataria, lindando de un lado a la Ultima Ysla, y del otro haciendo frente a la Ysla nombrado el Vino." [2]

Translated into English, Governor Miro's proclamation reads:

"To Jean Voisin, a small island, commonly called L'Isle Longue, situated in the Lake of Barrataria, adjoining (or contiguous to) on one side Last Island, and on the other, fronting the island called Wine Island." [3]

Throughout the 18th century, the promise of land attracted large numbers of settlers to the New World. No promise of that era was more enticing or more outlandish than that proffered by John Law, the architect of the *Mississippi Bubble*, the infamous 18th Century speculative debacle of that attracted large numbers of settlers to the New World. [4] This particular influx of humanity had its sights set on the rich, fertile lands of the lower Mississippi River Valley.

The use of land grants, of course, was not limited to John Law and his henchmen. During the last half of the 18th Century, Louisiana's French and Spanish provisional governors used their land grant authorities to encourage the settlement and development of the territory. While France and Spain both used land as a powerful enticement, each employed its strategies in markedly different ways.

For its part, the French government used the land grant authority to reward its powerful and wealthy benefactors. Spain's approach was much more practical and, in the end, infinitely more successful. Louisiana's Spanish provisional governors, such as Don Estevan Miro, were determined to attract as many settlers as possible. To achieve that goal, Spain chose to offer smaller tracts of land. Spain's math was quite simple – smaller grants meant more grants – and more grants sent large numbers of settlers streaming into the Lower Mississippi River Valley.

The Spanish governors added one other important incentive. They ensured that, where possible,

---

[2] *Public Land Claims, Number 4533*, National Archives and Records Administration, Washington DC.

[3] Ibid.

[4] John Law was the architect of the *Mississippi Bubble*. Law's manipulation of the several trading companies in Louisiana led eventually to the collapse of the *Banque Générale* – the central bank - in Paris. This event led to the devaluing of the shares Law had sold in the Mississippi Company. In the end, shares in the company were worthless and the financial community in France entered a prolonged period of financial stress.

the land grants would afford the settlers a degree of access to Louisiana's vital waterways. Few politicians articulated Spain's land grant policies more clearly than Baron Don Joseph Xavier de Pontalba.

"Louisiana wants working hands. Give her population and she will become an inexhaustible source of wealth…Give her population, whatever be the means employed. But give her population." [5]

By the end of the 18th century, Spain's land grant policies were an unqualified success. Settlers from Europe and the eastern seaboard regions of the United States streamed into the Lower Mississippi River region. Louisiana had its much-needed *"working hands."* One pair of those *"working hands"* belonged to Jean Voisin.

During the thirty-year period following issuance of his 1788 *Order of Survey*, Voisin divided his time between his small plantation on the west bank of the Mississippi River, south of New Orleans in the town of Pointe a la Haché, and a thriving fishing venture he had established on Isle Longue. The incredible quantity of fish and turtles caught in and around the island had but one objective and a singular destination – to satiate the demand for such delicacies in the markets and restaurants of New Orleans.

In the final years of the 18th century, life for Jean Voisin and his neighbors was predictable and mundane. The world around them, however, was about to change in ways that would be dramatic and breath-taking. At the center of the looming changes was Europe's most compelling military and political leader Napoléon Bonaparte. Emboldened by visions of a grand empire in the New World, Bonaparte had been pressuring Spain for the return of the Louisiana territory, which France had ceded to Spain only thirty years earlier. On October 1, 1800, the two European powers secretly signed the *Treaty of San Ildefonso*, which returned to France all territories west of the Mississippi River.

When word of the transfer leaked, United States President Thomas Jefferson became concerned for the well-being of the large numbers of American settlers in the area. In the spring of 1803, Jefferson dispatched then Governor of Virginia James Monroe to France. The President asked his one-time Minister to France to serve as envoy extraordinary and assist Robert Livingston, the United States' current Minister to France, in negotiating with the French. Jefferson's objective was a modest one. He wanted Monroe and Livingston to purchase the city of New Orleans and areas adjacent to the lower Mississippi River to the south of the city.

France, at this time, was bogged down in an ill-fated military campaign, one of many in a long string of such endeavors. Hostilities in Saint-Domingue (present-day Haiti) and France's continual state of war with England, made Bonaparte realize that his country's financial position was becoming increasingly untenable. The Emperor quickly realized that his government could not continue expending the resources needed to secure France's vast territories west of the Mississippi River.

---

[5] *History of Louisiana: the Spanish domination*, Charles Gayarré, 1867.

Bonaparte wasted little time in resolving his dilemma. He told his ministers to sell the entire Louisiana territory to the Americans. The offer of such a huge area caught Monroe and Livingston completely off guard. The two Americans, however, quickly recovered from their astonishment. Determined not to let such an extraordinary opportunity slip from their grasp, the American negotiators chose not to delay a decision in order to get prior approval from President Jefferson.

Monroe and Livingston immediately accepted the unprecedented offer. With the stroke of a pen, and an exchange of fifteen million dollars, the size of the United States doubled. The Louisiana Purchase added more than 800,000 square miles to the public domain.

The massive land transfer, however, did raise an important question. What was to be the status of those who had already settled in Louisiana, many of whom were Americans? To address the implications inherent in this question, a provision was inserted into Article Three of the 1803 Louisiana Purchase Treaty. It was a provision that ensured that all inhabitants of the Louisiana territory would retain their private ownership rights.

"Inhabitants of the ceded territory shall be incorporated in the Union of the United States and admitted as soon as possible according to the principles of the federal Constitution to the enjoyment of all these rights, advantages and immunities of citizens of the United States and in the mean time they shall be maintained and protected in the free enjoyment of their liberty, property and the Religion which they profess." [6]

For the settlers of the region, one phrase stood out. The landholders were to be *"...protected in the free enjoyment of their...property."* This unqualified commitment of the United States government enabled the hundreds of settlers in the newly acquired territory to continue clearing, cultivating and developing the region without fear of losing their properties to the state.

Because of the importance of New Orleans and the Lower Mississippi River Valley, Louisiana gained statehood in just over nine years. The change in status further strengthened the property rights of Louisiana's 76,000 inhabitants.

Jean Voisin enjoyed his new status for only a few more years. On August 10, 1820, the seventy year-old fisherman died. Surviving Jean Voisin were his two children – daughter Catherine and fifteen year-old Jean Joseph. Young Jean Joseph wasted little time in assuming responsibility for overseeing the day-to-day activities of the family on its west bank plantation near Pointe á la Hache and the highly profitable fishing enterprise on Isle Longue.

The transition from father to son had been a smooth one. How long, though, would that remain the case? A young Nation was changing dramatically and rapidly.

---

[6] *Louisiana Purchase Treaty, April 30, 1803* (ARC ID 299807), General Records of the United States Government, Record Group 11, National Archives and Records Administration

Chapter Two: Louisiana, a State in Transition

Life is pleasant. Death is peaceful. It's the transition that's troublesome.   - Isaac Asimov

The hundreds of land grants that had played such prominent role in populating Louisiana in the late 18th century left the fledgling American republic with a daunting challenge. How could the federal government validate those pre-existing land claims? United States land officials had more questions than answers.

Which lands were public? Which were private? If private, who was claiming the lands and on what basis? How large were those private claims and where were they located? Complicating the challenge of establishing a rational and workable land management system were the irregular, crude land measurement methods that had been cobbled together by France and Spain during their years of rule.

Over time, these antiquated land measurement systems would give way to an infinitely more uniform land survey system based on mathematics and a rectangular grid schema. The immediate challenge for United States land officials, particularly in areas that set astride the Mississippi River where the influences of French and Spanish provisional governments were so strong, was how to convert a surface measurement system based on *superficial arpents*, a basic measurement used by both European powers, to one based on *acres*.

In order to effectuate this crucial conversion, the federal government utilized survey practices defined by the Public Land Survey System (PLSS). The PLSS, which is rooted in the *Land Ordinance of 1785,* employs a land measurement methodology based on the square and its logical subdivisions. The new land survey system, for example, defined a township as a square area measuring six miles by six miles, or thirty-six square miles. Subdivided, each township consisted of thirty-six sections, with each section measuring one mile by one mile or 640 acres.

Through application of this and similar rules, the Public Land Survey System provided state and territorial land officials with a much-needed framework for administering the lands for which they were responsible. This was particularly true for land officials charged with administering lands obtained by virtue of the Louisiana Purchase. [7]

Not surprisingly, the continuing demand for land barely kept up with the numbers of settlers flooding into the new states and territories. To quench the public's insatiable thirst, the General Land Office (GLO) resorted to offering increasingly smaller sections of land. The GLO accomplished this by further subdividing each "*section*" of land into four 160-acre "*quarter sections*." The underlying genius of the PLSS' new measurement system is that each township was tailor-made for an endless string of standard subdivisions – sections, quarter sections, etc. The land survey system enabled the federal government to carry out land transactions, for the most part, in terms of whole acres.

Before long, land office officials were subdividing 160-acre quarter sections into 40-acre "*quarter-quarter*" sections. This particular unit of division served as the genesis for post-Civil

---

[7] *A History of the Rectangular Survey System*, C. Albert White, Department of the Interior, Bureau of Land Management, 1983

War references to *"40 acres and a mule,"* a phrase that is rooted in American history. [8]

Despite administering a proportional measurement system, land officials and surveyors were constantly beset with a myriad of problems - inaccuracies, poor instrumentation, hostile terrains, and generally unskilled or careless survey work. As a result, it was common for a section to deviate from the PLSS model of one square mile. In order to maintain as much uniformity as possible, the PLSS called for identifiable measurement errors to be pushed to the northwest corners of any effected townships. The land office's *"northwest corner"* approach kept measurement anomalies to a minimum and placing any detected deviations in a predictable location within a section. This solution ensured that at least three corners of a section or township was reasonably uniform.

While the standardized, proportional measurement methodology defined by the Public Land Survey System was conceptually sound, force fitting it atop the irregular land measurement systems practiced by the French and Spanish was fraught with difficulty and complexity. Converting Louisiana's superficial arpents to acres was particularly confusing for state land officials and land purchasers in south Louisiana, where pre-existing grants were typically long and narrow tracts of land with access to one or more of the state's vital waterways – and in south Louisiana, in particular, there were hundreds of bayous, rivers and lakes.

The merger of the two survey systems was, at best, a messy process but one that enabled the United States Government to effectively manage its rapidly expanding landscape. An important question, though, remained unanswered. How would the federal government finally resolve ownership issues involving the 18th century Spanish and French land grants?

To begin the process of answering such questions, the United States Congress established the General Land Office (GLO) in 1812. The federal land office was charged by Congress with overseeing and managing the westward expansion. To accomplish that, the GLO established a national board of land commissioners and a land commissioner for each state and territory. The General Land Office also mandated that each jurisdiction appoint a register, receiver, and surveyor general.

The new policies notwithstanding, administering the public land survey system was, more often than not, a laborious and confusing process. This was particularly true with respect to Louisiana, where, as late as 1830, much of the state remained uncharted. The status quo left hundreds of Louisiana's 18th century land grant holders in a prolonged state of uncertainty. On July 4, 1832, the United States Congress finally addressed this disquiet by passing *"An Act for the final adjustment of the claims to lands in the south-central land district of the State of Louisiana."* [9]

The legislation, long overdue, established a process by which 18th century land grant holders in

---

[8] The phrase *"forty acres and a mule"* is rooted in an action taken by General William T. Sherman in January 1865. In Special Field Order No. 15, Sherman committed to providing former slaves and their families with forty acres of land in South Carolina. Later, Sherman agreed to loan army mules to the settlers – from Eric Foner, *A Short History of Reconstruction, 1863-1877* (New York: Harper and Row, 1990).

[9] *Public Statutes at Large, Volume 1*, edited by Richard Peters, Little and Brown, Boston 1850

Louisiana could confirm their respective claims. The 1832 Act called for the submission of the original land grants to the State Register and Receiver. The State Register was responsible for reviewing and evaluating the documentation accompanying the submitted claims. The State Register was then required by the Act to send the assembled claims to the United States Secretary of the Treasury with a recommendation for each. The 1832 Act was very specific with respect to the actions required of the State Register and hundreds of land grant holders, one of which was Jean Joseph Voisin.

"Any persons claiming lands within the limits to the southeastern land district of the state of Louisiana…but whose titles have not been heretofore confirmed, may, at any time prior to the first day of July 1833, present their claims, together with the written evidence and other testimony in support of the same, to the register and receiver of the land office at New Orleans."

"It shall be the duty of the said register and receiver to record, in a book to be kept for that purpose, the notice of every claim so preferred, together with the evidence…" [10]

The 1832 Act continued, continued to outline the actions the State Register and Receiver were to take in submitting the claims.

"The said register and receiver shall, at or before the beginning of the next session of Congress…make to the Secretary of the Treasury, a report of the claims which have been preferred before them, together with the testimony, their opinion of the validity of the claims and such other information respecting them as may be in their possession…"

"[The]…report shall, by the Secretary of the Treasury, be laid before Congress as soon as practicable, with his opinion touching the validity of the respective claims." [11]

On July 1, 1833, Jean Joseph Voisin submitted documentation for two land claims to the State Land Office in New Orleans. One of voisin's claims was for a tract of land on the west bank of the Mississippi River, at Pointe á la Hache the other was for Isle Longue. Supporting Voisin's claim to the island was his copy of the original *Order of Survey* signed in 1788 by Spain's provisional governor, Don Estevan Miro. Also attached to his claim for Isle Longue was an affidavit sworn to by a Plaquemines Parish neighbor – Charles Carel.

"Charles Carel, being duly sworn deposith and saith that he is sixty-nine years of age, that he is well acquainted with the Island described in the above Order of Survey, and that the same was granted to Jean Voisin…That from the time of the Confirmation, it has always been in his possession or in that of those who held it for him." [12]

For nearly two months, Louisiana Register Hilary Cenas pored over more than three hundred land claims, carefully evaluating the supporting documents for each. On September 5, 1833, the State Register forwarded the land claims and his accompanying recommendation for each to the

---

[10] Ibid.

[11] Ibid.

[12] *Public Land Claims, Number 4533*, National Archives and Records Administration, Washington DC.

General Land Office in Washington. The GLO was responsible for reviewing and approving the recommendations before forwarding the collection of land claims to the Secretary of the Treasury.

Register Cenas, as required by the 1832 Act, classified the three hundred-plus land claims in four separate claims categories – A, B, C and D.

Class A claims included *"claims founded upon grants or concessions made and completed n due form by the French or Spanish governments."*

Class B included *"claims founded upon incomplete titles, such as orders or warrants of survey, authentic surveys, etc."*

Class C consisted of *"claims founded upon possession and cultivation for at least ten consecutive years prior to the 20th day of December, 1803."*

The final category, Class D, included a small number of *"claims described in the 4th section of the act of July 4, 1832."* [13]

The two claims submitted by Jean Joseph Voisin were classified as *"Class B"* claims and labeled *"B. Number 49"* and *"B. Number 50."*

On January 9, 1834, General Land Office Commissioner Elijah Hayward completed his review of the Register's recommendations and forwarded the documents to Secretary of the Treasury Roger B. Taney. Included in the report to the Secretary was a recommendation for each land claim, including his approval of Jean Joseph Voisin's two requests.

"B. Number 49 – Jean Voisin claims a tract of land situate in the parish of Plaquemines, and on the west bank of the river Mississippi, containing five arpents [front] by the ordinary depth of forty arpents, and bounded above by land of ...Latour, Jr., and below by land of Anseline Arnaud."

"The said tract of land is claimed by virtue of ancient and undisputed possession, having been constantly and uninterruptedly inhabited and cultivated, by claimant and those under whom he holds, for the last forty years and upwards, three arpents front thereof being derived by purchase from one Jacques Nivet, who obtained an order of survey therefore from the Baron de Carondelet, on the 12th day of December, 1796."

"We are, therefore, of opinion that this claim ought to be confirmed."

"B. Number 50 - Jean Voisin claims another tract of land being a small island situated in the lake of Barataria (parish of Jefferson) and commonly called L'Ile Congue (sic) containing about six hundred superficial arpents and fronting on one side another island called El Vino."

---

[13] *Public Statutes at Large, Volume 1*, edited by Richard Peters, Little and Brown, Boston 1850.

"The said island is claimed in virtue of a regular order of survey issued thereof in favor of said claimant, by Governor Estevan Miro, on the 3rd (sic) day of October, 1788, and of continued occupation and possession thereof ever since."

"We are therefore of opinion that this claim ought to be confirmed." [14]

Three weeks later, on January 31, 1834, Treasury Secretary Taney reviewed and concurred with each Cenas' recommendations. Taney, who would become Chief Justice of the Supreme Court of the United States in 1836, bundled up the approved claims and forwarded them to the United States Speaker of the House of Representatives, Andrew Stevenson of the Commonwealth of Virginia.

"Sir: I have the honor herewith to transmit the original report of the register and receiver of the land office at New Orleans, made pursuant to the act of Congress approved July 4, 1832, entitled 'An act for the final adjustment of the claims to lands in the southeastern land district of the State of Louisiana.'" [15]

Taney's letter to the Speaker noted that *"the register and receiver shall, at or before the beginning of the next session of Congress...make to the Secretary of the Treasury a report of the claims...together with the testimony, their opinion of the validity of the claims, and such other information respecting them as may be in their possession; which report shall, by the Secretary of the Treasury, be laid before congress as soon as practical, with hs opinion touching the validity of the respective claims."*

"The evidence in support of the several claims not having been forwarded to the department as required by the act, I have not therefore the testimony which would enable me to form an opinion of the validity of the respective claims; moreover, it would require more time to examine them with proper care than could be given to the subject consistently with the other duties during the present session of Congress."

"Under these circumstances, as delay may be injurious to the interests of the public as well as the individuals, I have deemed it my duty to communicated to Congress the report of the register and receiver, and to submit to their judgment....I have the honor also to transmit the remarks of the Commissioner of the General Land Office on several of the claims mentioned in the report of the register and receiver. All [of] which is respectfully submitted. (signed) R. B. Taney, Secretary of the Treasury" [16]

Taney's recommendation to confirm the hundreds of land claims reached Congress well in advance of the date prescribed in the law. Fourteen months later, the 23rd Session of the House of Representatives passed the concluding portion of the 1832 legislation - an Act aimed at *"finally adjusting"* the many private land claims carried over from Louisiana's pre-statehood

---

[14] *American State Papers: Volume 6, Public Lands, Land Claims in Louisiana*, pages 667-702

[15] *"An Act for the final adjustment of the claims to land in the southeastern district of Louisiana, March 3, 1835 (4 Statute 779, 780)"* – from *American State Papers: Volume 6*, pages 665ff

[16] Ibid.

days.

On March 3, 1835, the United States House of Representatives confirmed the claims with the passage of a Bill that was *"supplementary to the act of the fourth of July, eighteen hundred and thirty-two, entitled 'An act for the final adjustment of the claims of lands in the southeastern district of Louisiana.'"* [17]   The confirming language was precise and unambiguous.

"Be it enacted...that the claims for lands within the southeastern district of the state of Louisiana, described by the register and receiver of the said district, in their report to the secretary of the treasury, bearing date the fifth of September, eighteen hundred and thirty-three, at New Orleans, be, and the same are hereby confirmed against any claim on the part of the United States..."[18]

Nearly forty-seven years had passed since the Governor Miro had issued his Order of Survey to Jean Voisin.   At long last, by virtue of the 1835 Act of Congress, Isle Longue was officially the property of Jean Joseph Voisin – or was it?

Chapter Three: "Now you see it...Now you don't!"

The magician and the politician have much in common: they both have to draw our attention away from what they are really doing. - Ben Okri, Nigerian Poet

---

[17] Ibid.

[18] Ibid.

For Jean Joseph Voisin and his neighbors, the years following 1835 – the year in which Congress finally passed the Act that confirmed the decades old French and Spanish land grants - were years of relative tranquility and routine. Voisin continued to do what he had been doing since his father's death in 1820, indeed, he continued to do as his father had done for years. The thirty year-old fisherman and farmer divided his time between overseeing the family plantation near Pointe á la Hache and managing a thriving fishing enterprise on Isle Longue.

Given the fact that Isle Longue was located seventy miles to the west and accessible only by boat, the day-to-day oversight of the fishing operation evolved over time into a loosely constructed partnership between two families – the Voisins and Dinets. The arrangement had been in place since the earliest years of the 19th century, when Jean Voisin first hooked up with Pierre Dinet.

Working together, the two men established a small fishing camp on the west end of the island. To run their modest enterprise, Voisin and Dinet placed three or four men on the island to maintain the camp day to day and fish and trap the surrounding areas. To ensure their wishes were carried out as intended, Voisin and Dinet travel to Isle Longue periodically to check on the men and their camp. At the end of each visit, the two partners would load the latest catches of redfish, oysters, turtles and other delicacies onto their boat and transport the haul to the bustling markets of New Orleans.

Historical accounts of the business arrangement suggest that the two men would, at times, travel to Isle Longue together and, at other times, travel separately. The Isle Longue partnership passed seamlessly to Jean Joseph Voisin following the death of his father in 1820. For the better part of two decades, young Jean Joseph Voisin's life was unchanging and predictable

In sharp contrast, State Land Office officials in Louisiana in the mid-1830s were facing a staggering challenge. The Surveyor General wrestled fiercely with the daunting task of surveying more than fifty thousand square miles to the west of the Mississippi River. The job of mapping Louisiana and laying out the required grid of townships and sections was a slow, tedious and oft-confusing process. Managing the public domain for a rapidly expanding nation required the services of scores of surveyors and deputy surveyors.

In November 1837, Henry T. Williams, Surveyor General of Public Lands for the State of Louisiana, contracted with one such deputy - Gilmore F. Connelly – to survey the southern portions of Terrebonne Parish, including "…*all the islands on the coast within those limits*." [19]

Connelly spent nearly three months surveying the southernmost reaches of Terrebonne Parish, completing the coastal portion of his assigned surveys in early February 1838. A few weeks later, Connelly delivered his completed survey plats and field notes to the Surveyor General's Office in Donaldsonville. Included in his collection of survey plats were several that delineated

---

[19] Last Island Survey Plats - Bureau of Land Management, Eastern States Office, Cadastral Survey Division, Springfield VA

17

the State's three westernmost barrier islands - Last Island, Wine Island and Caillou Island. With so many more surveys still to be completed, Louisiana's land officials just added the Connelly surveys to a rapidly growing stack of documents.

Nearly five years passed before officials in the State Land Office got around to reviewing Connelly's 1838 survey documents. Following a quick, perfunctory review, a land office official hastily annotated each of Connelly's four survey plats for Last Island – the inscription read simply *"received and certified, December 8, 1842."* [20]

As land officials in Donaldsonville had been doing for the past four years, the survey plats and surveyor notes were simply placed on a shelf with hundreds of other completed surveys. Connelly's survey of the barrier islands off the Terrebonne Parish coast remained there, undisturbed for another eighteen months. The documents' period of dormancy was interrupted ever-so briefly in 1844 by the insertion of a second annotation to – a tersely written four-word entry that was destined to alter the status of land on the west end of Last Island.

"Subject to private entry – July 15, 1844." [21]

Last Island was for sale. The island's availability status may have changed in 1844 but few people in south Louisiana were even aware of that fact. Once again, officials in the Surveyor General's Office simply annotated the status change and re-filed the documents. The survey plats remained undisturbed for another four years, retrieved only when a St. Mary Parish sugar planter inquired about buying a strip of land on the west end of the island – an island he knew as Last Island.

On April 8, 1848, Thomas Maskell purchased four tracts of land, totaling one hundred and sixty acres. The property was located approximately six miles to the east of the island's western tip – Raccoon Point. Three months later, on July 13, 1848, the State Land Office sold a second parcel of land. James Nixon Wafford acquired a fifty-three-acre tract just to the west of Maskell's recent acquisition. Maskell paid the State $200.08 for his one hundred and sixty acres. The Wafford purchase, the smaller of the two, cost only $66.25. The two transactions, totaling a sum of two hundred and sixty-six dollars and thirty-three cents, were about to change the face and the future of the island. [22]

It is not clear when Voisin first learned of the sales. He may have gotten wind of the purchases during the last half of 1848. He clearly was aware of the transactions before the spring of 1849 and, as soon as he did learn, a highly agitated Jean Joseph Voisin wasted little time. He immediately confronted Maskell and Wafford, waving his documents in the face of each man. Voisin exclaimed that he was the owner of the island. His *"proof"* consisted of copies of the 1788 *Order of Survey*, which initially granted the island to his father, and the 1835 Act of Congress, by which the United States Government had formally confirmed his ownership of the

---

[20] Ibid.

[21] Ibid.

[22] Record of Sales on Last Island from the *Bethany Bultman Collection*, Historic New Orleans Collection, New Orleans LA.

island.

Not surprisingly, Thomas Maskell and James Wafford were prepared with their own responses. The two men countered Voisin's assertions with their own ownership documents, land titles recently issued by the State Land Office. Voisin's continuing and persistent protests – protests that grew more strident with each passing month – were for naught.

In a completely unrelated move, the United States Congress on March 2, 1849, passed the *Swamp and Overflowed Land Grant Act.* The legislation was designed *"to aid the State of Louisiana in draining the Swamp Lands therein."* [23] The Act coincidentally and conveniently served another objective. It was tailor-made for the actions the State Land Office in Louisiana wanted to take with respect to Last Island. Within days of passage, the land office designated Last Island as *"swamp land."*

This new designation, combined with the surging popularity of the island, precipitated a flurry of sales inquiries. In a single month - July 1849 - the State Land Office completed ten more transactions, totaling 312 acres. Three months later, the State sold another eight tracts, totaling 341 acres. By October, 1849, almost nine hundred acres, nearly two-thirds of Last Island's prized west end, were in the hands of men who had but one thing on their minds – creating the South's most desirous summer destination.

Congress clearly did not pass the *Swamp and Overflowed Land Grant Act* just to facilitate the sale of land on Last Island. In fact, the legislation was intended to assist a dozen or more states and territories in more effectively managing and placing into private hands their respective *"swamp lands."* Last Island may not have been the objective of the Act but it clearly became a means to an end for the State Land Office.

Whatever the motivation of state land officials, one thing was clear, in less than six months, most of the island's coveted beachfront was in private hands. Not surprisingly, the two rounds of land sales in 1849, accompanied by the subsequent construction and development activity, fueled the public's interest in the west end's remaining acreage.

Jean Joseph Voisin continued to protest the sales throughout 1849. With one notable exception, his protests fell on deaf ears. On July 26, 1849, Alexander Pope Field had used a military land warrant [24] to secure more than one hundred acres on Last Island. Only a few years earlier, Field, a renowned Illinois trial attorney and politician, was embroiled in one of the Nation's most politically-charged and highly contentious trials – the landmark Dred Scott case. As co-counsel to Dred Scott, the Kentucky-born, pro-slavery Field was trapped professionally in an awkward position. When his co-counsel died unexpectedly, Field jumped at the opportunity to withdraw from the case. For Alexander Field, it was a perfect time to put his military warrant to good use and an enticing tract of land on Last Island seemed the perfect fit.

---

[23] *Swamp and Overflowed Lands in the United States, Ownership and Reclamation*, by J. O. Wright, United States Department of Agriculture, Government Printing Office, Washington DC 1907.

[24] Military land warrants (also known as Bounty Land Warrants) were granted by the United States Government from the colonial period to 1858 to attract men into the Army or to reward them for their services.

Just as he had done with the title claims of Maskell and Wafford, Jean Joseph Voisin immediately challenged the legitimacy of Field's warrant. The Kentuckian listened patiently to Voisin and then decided to approach Louisiana Surveyor General R. W. Boyd for a ruling. In a letter dated August 6, 1849, Alexander Field explained that he had been on Last Island but a short time when Voisin, with papers in hand, approached him, insisting that he [Voisin] was the rightful owner of the island. Determined to head off any legal complications over ownership, Field asked for Boyd's guidance.

"Please give me your opinion as to whether my claim is sufficiently clear...to warrant its location." [25]

A short time later, Surveyor General Boyd responded, explaining to Field that while the State Land Office maintained the survey plats for Last Island and other barrier islands, his office had no records related to a survey of Isle Longue. Boyd continued, noting that Connelly's 1838 Last Island survey plats and field notes contained no references whatsoever to an Isle Longue. Jean Joseph Voisin's predicament, which was worsening by the day, was increasingly defined by a single question.

"Where was Isle Longue?"

When Voisin had applied for and received Congressional confirmation of his claim to Isle Longue in 1835, no one asked such a question. Jean Joseph Voisin had played by all the rules. Now, fifteen years later, Voisin found himself ensnared by a bureaucratic version of *Three Card Monte*.

Voisin well knew the location of his *"queen of hearts"* – Isle Longue. The crafty bureaucrats in the office of the Louisiana Surveyor General, however, were deftly moving the survey plats for the barrier islands face down about the table. With a *"légèreté des mains"* – a *"lightness of the hands"* – that would have impressed the most accomplished French Quarter street hustler, officials at the State Land Office teased Jean Joseph Voisin with a hurried glimpse of what he believed to be the Isle Longue *"card."* The officials then returned it to its face down position.

The next move would belong to Voisin. Unlike sleight of hand routines in the *Vieux Carré* that play out in the blink of an eye, the puzzling disappearance of Isle Longue was stretched out over an extended period of years. Like most marks, Jean Joseph Voisin was unaware of the high-stakes game he had joined, unaware of the well-dressed, well-spoken shills in the State Land Office, unaware of the switch of the islands.

For Jean Joseph Voisin, things had been so simple, so very innocent.

"Just keep your eye on Isle Longue."

"Now you see it..."

---

[25] *Public Land Claims, Number 4533*, National Archives and Records Administration, Washington DC.

In 1849, Jean Joseph Voisin presented his confirmation papers to Maskell and Wafford. Did they not know they were on his island? Did they not know they were own Isle Longue?

Ninety miles away, the Surveyor General for the State of Louisiana slowly turned face up each of several survey plats for Terrebonne Parish. There were the surveys for Last Island. There, too, were the surveys for Wine Island and Caillou Island. Voisin watched the game played out.

"...and now you don't!"

On his lips, a single question lingered. It was a question that one hundred and sixty years later still lingered, still begged for an answer.

"Where WAS Isle Longue?"

Chapter Four: Opening Salvos

"After a spell, a lot of fellers come out...and they all laid their heads together

like as many lawyers when they are gettin' ready to prove that a man's heirs ain't got any right to his property." - Thomas Jefferson Snodgrass, from a letter to the Keokuk *Saturday Post*, November 1, 1856

Jean Joseph Voisin's perplexed looks and probing questions did little to dampen the mushrooming fascination with the island. Increasing numbers of south Louisianans simply wanted in on the action, each wanting his own personal connection to the emerging jewel of Terrebonne Parish. Rebuffed repeatedly by Thomas Maskell and James Wafford and further frustrated by the subsequent swarm of "*swamp land*" speculators, Voisin turned to the mainland for legal advice.

Attorney F. C. Laville carefully examined his new client's documents and then settled thoughtfully on his course of action. He began by questioning the three central land officials - Louisiana Surveyor General Robert W. Boyd, State Register Gideon Fitz and General Land Office Commissioner Justin Butterfield. Laville wrote to each man and asked for the status of Jean Joseph Voisin's confirmed land claim. In his letters, Laville made a point to ask a question the land officials were dodging.

"*When can Jean Joseph Voisin expect to receive his patent for Isle Longue?*"

Months passed without a single reply. Laville at least understood the reason for the procrastination in the State Land Office. He surmised that officials there were far too busy selling off the remaining acreage on the island's coveted west end. A full year would pass before all three men had answered Laville's letters. The General Land Office Commissioner was first to reply.

Justin Butterfield told Laville that he had written to Boyd on April 26, 1850, requesting the status of Voisin's confirmed claim. Two weeks later, Boyd's responded to the GLO commissioner's request. Louisiana's Surveyor General advised Butterfield that while Jean Joseph Voisin may hold a claim that was confirmed by Congress fifteen years earlier, an island by the name of Isle Longue "*has not yet been surveyed, nor has any order for its location been issued by this office.*"[26]

Boyd inserted one other observation into his letter - "*...the only townships adjoining Lake Barataria which have had surveys are Townships 19 and 21 and upon these no islands of the name L'Isle Longue appear to have been surveyed.*"

That one sentence contained the word that would forever define the Isle Longue controversy - "*Barataria.*"

As far as the State Land Office was concerned, if an Isle Longue did exist – or ever existed - it could only be found miles to the east of Last Island in or around Barataria Bay. Boyd's contention that "*no islands of the name L'Isle Longue appear to have been surveyed,*" failed to

---

[26] *Public Land Claims, Number 4533*, National Archives and Records Administration, Washington DC.

deter Laville or his client Jean Joseph Voisin. Laville's explanation was a simple one. The name Isle Longue had given way over time to the more familiar appellation - *L' Isle Derniere* or Last Island. The Laville arguments, however, fell upon deaf ears.

Boyd's dismissive response did not, however, deter GLO Commissioner Butterfield, who was simultaneously pressing the issue with Louisiana State Register Gideon Fitz. Butterfield instructed Fitz to prepare a detailed assessment of the case, in general, and Laville's assertions, in particular, and send that report to the land office in Washington.

To Butterfield's chagrin, the Louisiana State Register's stance was even more rigid than that exhibited by Boyd. Writing to Butterfield on September 5, 1850, Fitz caustically characterized Voisin's claim to Last Island as *"frivolous."*

"The area now known as Last Island is too big to be the small island described in the Order of Survey...[the] Order of Survey grants an island bounded on one side by 'Last Island' and so it cannot mean Last Island itself."

The State Register's assessment continued to skirt the increasingly obvious question.

"If Last Island and Isle Longue are not one and the same island, where then is Isle Longue?" [27]

The adversaries of Jean Joseph Voisin exhibited little interest in determining the precise location of Isle Longue. Did they fear that such an effort might cast a cloud of uncertainty over the skyrocketing popularity of Last Island? The State Land Office seemed much too eager to sidestep such questions. This was simply not the time to challenge the legitimacy of the recently sanctioned land transactions. The position taken by both Boyd and Fitz was one that was unquestionably favorable to Maskell, Wafford and a dozen other powerful interests.

The back and forth discussions and correspondence continued unabated well into 1851. Laville peppered Fitz and Butterfield relentlessly with the demands of his client. Voisin's attorney repeatedly pressed the issue by pointing to the two central documents in the case – Governor Don Estevan Miro's 1788 *Order of Survey* and the 1835 Act of Congress, which confirmed Voisin's claim to the island. In every exchange, Laville demanded an answer to the one question the land officials were dodging.

"Where is Jean Joseph Voisin's title to Isle Longue?

Louisiana State Register Fitz, who was fast tiring of the endless barrage of charges and counter-charges, wrote once again to Butterfield. On January 6, 1852, the man who had initially dismissed Voisin's claim as *"frivolous"* finally relented and agreed to prepare a comprehensive summary of the dispute for the General Land Office. Frustrated by the foot-dragging of land officials in Louisiana and Washington, F. C. Laville was busily drafting his own detailed account of events and unresolved issues.

---

[27] Ibid.

Laville prepared a lengthy chronology, which included an assortment of relevant facts, dates, sworn affidavits and a surprisingly detailed map of Isle Longue and Last Island that he had sketched during the summer of 1851. Determined to bolster the credibility of his client, Laville took every opportunity to explain apparent inconsistencies and contradictions.

"It is proper that in concluding this history of Voisin's title, we should notice an apparent discrepancy between the original order of survey and the recommendation for confirmation upon which our adversaries appear to depend very much; it is this: the original Spanish order of survey…fixes fully the location of Isle Longue by stating that on one side it is contiguous to Last Island and that on the other it fronts Wine Island; while in the recommendation for confirmation, the first of these boundaries to wit Last Island, (la Ultima Isla) is not mentioned and the second to wit El Vino (Wine Island) is the only one stated." [28]

He attributed many of the cited discrepancies to *"want of a complete knowledge of the Spanish language"* or *"mere clerical error."* Laville then pointed to what he considered one of the strengths of Jean Joseph Voisin's argument.

In 1834, when the Louisiana State Register and Receiver sent their formal recommendation to United States Secretary of the Treasury Roger B. Taney, they described Isle Longue as being adjacent to Wine Island. As far as Voisin attorney F. C. Laville was concerned, this declaration placed Isle Longue squarely in the coastal waters of Terrebonne Parish. Laville reminded Butterfield that at no point during the three-year confirmation process – a process mandated by Congress – were the documents submitted by Jean Joseph Voisin ever questioned. The attorney's confidence in his client was unwavering.

"We need not…feel uneasy about it."

Laville, of course, could not explain every discrepancy. One was the puzzling reference to the *"Parish of Jefferson,"* which had been added parenthetically to the State Register's 1834 recommendation.

"What they meant by that, we cannot account for. Certainly it is not in the original Spanish Order of Survey."

Laville repeatedly and confidently pointed to the 1835 Congressional Act, which confirmed Voisin's claim to Isle Longue.

"From what precedes, we apprehend that Voisin's title is fully made out…as required by Law."

To further reinforce his confidence in his client's position, Laville quoted from Louisiana State Register Hilary Cenas' initial 1834 recommendation.

"We are happy to state that in no instance has an attempt been made to impose upon us a claim which has not been of a character to stand successfully…"

---

[28] Ibid.

Laville suggested that the passage of the *Swamp Lands Act* in 1849 served only to confuse matters.

"Towards the years 1848, which Voisin was quietly residing with his family on his island, to wit, Isle Longue, the United States Land Surveyor treating Voisin's property as vacant land belonging to the Government, came and surveyed what they pretended to call Last Island, and included under that name, not only Last Island...[but] Isle Longue...and [designated them the Swamp Lands...making a swamp of the whole..."

Laville reminded the commissioner of the General Land Office that the first land transactions – the 1848 sales to Wafford and Maskell - occurred a full thirteen years after Congress had confirmed his client's claim to the island. The attorney's entreaty concluded with a fervent appeal.

"Voisin is a good and honest man but he is also a very ignorant man. It was only when he saw so many neighbors flocking around him, that he began to open his eyes, and ventured some observations to those who were taking possession of his property, which were treated with contempt. [Voisin] claims only what was granted by Governor Miro...our adversaries appear to be little disposed to do us justice..." [29]

Laville's impassioned protests and pleas notwithstanding, the General Land Office continued to procrastinate. Months passed and still Laville had no further word from Washington. The rhythm of the dispute was growing increasingly more frustrating and more predictable. The unresponsiveness of the two land agencies continued to leave open the door to still more land sales on the island. The door did not remain open for long. In one final flurry of activity in 1852, the remaining acreage on Last Island was sold.

As of May 6, 1852, the entire west end of Jean Joseph Voisin's island was in private hands. As soon as he got wind of this final round of sales, Laville loosed another round of letters to the General Land Office, demanding that the agency make a decision in the case. Growing weary of the Washington run-around, Jean Joseph Voisin's attorney began writing to members of the Louisiana delegation in Congress. On July 28, 1852, he wrote to United States Senator Pierre Soulé and pleaded for congressional intervention in the dispute.

More months passed and still no response from the General Land Office. Eventually, Laville learned of at least one reason for Washington's unresponsiveness. Butterfield's term as GLO commissioner had ended. On September 16, 1852, John Wilson took the oath of office as the new head of the General Land Office.

News of the leadership change in Washington persuaded Laville to resume his letter-writing campaign. In November 1852, he wrote to Commissioner Wilson and demanded a decision regarding the status of Jean Joseph Voisin's claim – a decision he had been unable to extract from Butterfield.

---

[29] Ibid.

As frustrating as the bureaucratic inaction was to Laville and his client, it was music to the ears of more than a dozen new Last Island patent holders. Their determination to develop Last Island had gone completely unchecked. With the exception of a single fisherman – Jean Joseph Voisin – who went about the island protesting that their presence on his island, the new *"owners"* had what they had been seeking. They had their slice of Louisiana's island paradise. On June 15, 1853, a frustrated, exasperated F. C. Laville wrote again to Washington, complaining to GLO Commissioner Wilson.

"I has [sic] written thrice requesting a decision."

Four more months passed without any word. Finally, on October 10, 1853, the federal behemoth began to stir. Commissioner Wilson wrote to New Orleans and directed that newly appointed State Register Louis Palms *"make a final examination of the matter after due notice to all the parties interested and to report the result for a definitive action of this office."*

Palms immediately began deposing witnesses. By February 1, 1854, the State Register had completed an initial round of examinations. Four weeks later, on February 28, he and Receiver Henry W. Palfrey submitted their report to Wilson.

"Sir, pursuant to instructions from your Office dated 10ᵗʰ of October 1853, Jean Voisin on the one part, and the State of Louisiana - David R. Muggah, James N. Wafford, Pinkney C. Bethel, Thomas Maskell, Elias Beers, Alex Leon, fields and others who acquired title to certain land on Last Island from the United States were notified to appear at this office on the 28ᵗʰ day of January 1854 with evidence in support of their respective claims." [30]

"All the parties are represented by counsel." [31]

Palms' report included copies of Voisin's 1788 *Order of Survey*, the State Register's 1834 recommendation to the Secretary of the Treasury and Congress in support of Jean Joseph Voisin, and the 1835 Act of Congress that confirmed Voisin's claim. The State Register also included a copy of a second *Order of Survey*, issued in 1788 by Spanish Provisional Governor Don Estevan Miro. This second *Order of Survey* had been issued to Juan Chapa for an island called Brush Island, which was described in the document as being located in Lake Barataria.

State Register Louis Palms confirmed to the GLO that Brush Island was well-known and was located to the west of Bayou Lafourche, only a short distance from Wine Island.

Outlining the arguments against Jean Joseph Voisin, State Register Palms included references to the 1838 survey plats, which had been the basis for selling what remained of the west end under authority of the 1849 *Swamp and Overflowed Land Grant Act*. His voluminous report also included numerous affidavits, each supporting one side of the dispute or the other. In March 1854, the thick case file reached the desk of General Land Office Commissioner John Wilson.

---

[30] Ibid.

[31] Ibid.

Surprising none of the parties back in Louisiana, the report remained there untouched for months.

In Terrebonne Parish, the waiting was over. The principle combatants had tired of the federal government's filibustering. James Wafford was the first to act.

By 1854, Jean Joseph Voisin had grown frustrated but so too had his principle adversary, James Nixon Wafford, who had wearied of the unceasing accusations. The two men were clearly destined for a moment of reckoning. The breaking point came when a flustered Voisin decided to move his entire family from their plantation near Pointe á la Hache to the island. Accusations were one thing, but particularly enraging to Wafford was the fact that Voisin began building on the tract of land that the St. Mary sugar planter had "*purchased*" from the State Land Office.

The standoff between the two men, which had been simmering for five years, had finally boiled over on September 25, 1854. On that early fall Monday, James Wafford instructed his attorney, Gilmore F. Connelly, to file suit with Terrebonne Parish Deputy Clerk Aubin Bourg. Petition Number 1824 spelled out the case against Jean Joseph Voisin.

"*The petition of James N. Wafford...would respectfully show that he is the legal owner of a tract of land...at a place known as Last Island...[Township 24, Range 15 East, Lot 1, containing 53 acres]...purchased...on July 13, 1848...*"

"*Your petitioner would further state that one Jean Voisin...has without the shadow of title or right, taken possession of his said tract of land and refuses to deliver [it]...Voisin pretends to be the owner...slanders the title of your petitioner...to deprive him of all chance of selling the [land] and by his illegal possession, preventing petitioner from privacy and occupying said tract of land to his great damage and hurt, at least $1,000.*" [32]

Wafford's petition estimated the value for his fifty-three acres to be "*at least $8,000.*" The suit outlined Wafford's repeated efforts to order Voisin and his family off of his [Wafford's] land "*but without avail.*" The petition sought two outcomes. One was that the Voisins be promptly evicted from Wafford's property. The second demand was for an assessment of "*damages for his* [Voisin's] *illegal acts.*"

The following day, the Fifth Judicial District Court issued a summons for Jean Joseph Voisin to appear in district court. Voisin was to respond in writing to the Clerk of Court in Houma within ten days of receipt of the summons. On October 4, 1854, Terrebonne Parish Sheriff Joseph A. Gagne traveled by boat to Last Island and delivered the warrant in person. Upon his arrival, however, Gagne learned that Jean Joseph Voisin was not at home.

Undeterred, Gagne left the summons with Voisin's wife. A few days later, an official in Terrebonne Parish Clerk of Court's office realized that the summons was invalid because it had not been hand-delivered to Jean Joseph Voisin. Deputy Clerk of Court Bourg ordered a second attempt, one that wound up taking five weeks to accomplish. To the chagrin of Wafford and his

---

[32] *Public Land Claims, Number 4533*, National Archives and Records Administration, Washington DC.

Last Island neighbors, the delay gave Voisin's attorneys time to prepare their own counter measures.

The Wafford summons was officially received by Jean Joseph Voisin on November 28, 1854. On that same day, Voisin attorneys John Randolph Grymes, Jr.[33] and Charles A. Maurian were in Houma filing a counter suit, in which they named James Wafford and other "*so-called*" patent holders as defendants.

"Jean Joseph Voisin…comes into this Honorable Court…and protests…[Mr. Voisin] asks…that the petition [of Mr. Wafford] be dismissed…Voisin denies generally all and singular the averments and allegations of…[Mr. Wafford]." [34]

The counter-suit declared that Jean Joseph Voisin was the "*true and lawful owner*" of the island that, according to the attorneys, had been "*wrongfully*" called Last Island. As they had done so many times before, Voisin's attorneys produced copies of the three documents that, in their collective judgment, clearly established Voisin's claims of ownership – the 1788 *Order of Survey*, the 1833 Register's recommendation to the United States Secretary of the Treasury, and the 1835 Act of Congress confirming his claim to Isle Longue.

The documentation filed with the district court included a personal affidavit that affirmed the Voisins "*continued possession*" of the island for more than fifty years. Voisin's counter-petition asked that Wafford's "*demand be dismissed…[and] that this respondent[Voisin] be declared to be the owner of the land described.*" [35]

In a thrust designed to raise the legal ante, Grymes and Maurian asked the court to order Wafford to pay Voisin damages totaling $3,000. Opposing attorneys in the case focused first on perfecting their respective cases. To strengthen Wafford's petition, attorney G. F. Connelly added several other Last Island patent holders as co-plaintiffs.

Attorneys for the two sides spent the next several months identifying and deposing witnesses and preparing their respective interrogatories and cross-interrogatories. Unwilling to rely solely on the efforts of his attorney, Thomas Maskell, who had purchased the first tracts of land on April 8, 1848, embarked on his own letter-writing campaign, beginning with the General Land Office in Washington. In his March 2, 1855, letter to GLO Commissioner John Wilson, Thomas Maskell got right to the point.

"I hold a patent to a tract of land on Last Island that Voisin is claiming." [36]

A week later, he mailed a similar letter to Louisiana State Register Louis Palms. In the letter, Maskell urged Palms to make his own inquiries of the General Land Office. Unlike Palms'

---

[33] Sixty-eight year-old John Randolph Grymes, Jr. died less than one week later on December 4, 1854. Voisin replaced Grymes with attorney Miles Taylor III.

[34] *Public Land Claims, Number 4533*, National Archives and Records Administration, Washington DC.

[35] Ibid.

[36] Ibid.

predecessor - Gideon Fitz – the new State Register was eager for the GLO to resolve the dispute once and for all. As attorneys prepared for the upcoming legal battle, more letters were dispatched to Washington.

Not to be outdone, two of Voisin's attorneys – Miles Taylor and H. H. Taylor - wrote to Commissioner Wilson on April 2, 1855, echoing the State Register's demands for a timely resolution to the dispute. By mid-April, attorneys for the opposing sides had submitted their proposed interrogatories to the court. The court allotted an additional three days for the adversaries to prepare their respective cross-interrogatories. On April 17, 1855, Fifth District Court Judge James Coles commissioned all judicial authorities in New Orleans to depose Voisin's first six witnesses - Jerome Moreno, Jean Pierre Catour, Jean Petit, F. C. Laville, Pierre Bromen and Lucien Dinet.

The district judge requested written depositions from each of the six witnesses and ordered that, upon receipt, the statements be forwarded to courthouse in Houma within the month. Nine days later, the judge added a seventh name to Voisin's list –Jean Baptiste Benate. During the second week of May 1855, Justice of the Peace Richard Richardson of New Orleans forwarded the depositions of Pierre Bromen, Jean Pierre Catour and Jerome Moreno to Houma. Judge Coles carefully studied the depositions, slowly forming a mental picture of the dispute. The litigation was about to enter a new phase, one that promised an end to the contentious, bitter legal contest between men of modest means and those of influence.

On one side were Jean Joseph Voisin and his supporters, simple men trying to help one of their own hold on to a piece of land lawfully granted by Spain's provisional government more than sixty years earlier. On the other side was an assemblage of some of Louisiana's wealthiest, most powerful men. It promised to be a battle of fishermen and kings.

Voisin's attorney, F. C. Laville, described his client as *"a good and honest man but…also a very ignorant man."* [37] Laville contended that Voisin learned too late that a group of wealthy planters and politicians had begun buying up the island, tract by tract, acre by acre. Voisin's attorney passionately argued that his client's family had owned and possessed the island for more than sixty years. Voisin had spent the past five years confronting his adversaries armed only with his copies of the 1788 *Order of Survey* and a twenty year-old Act of Congress. This time, the testimony of others would join Voisin's fight. The question, though, was whether the voices of a group of old men – comprised largely of fishermen and pilots – would be carry the day.

The fishermen were the first to take the stand.

Chapter Five: Fishermen…

"We shall walk in pleasant vales, listening to the shepherd's song. I shall tell him lovely tales all day long. He shall laugh while mother sings tales of fishermen and kings." - Fred Noyes, *Forty Singing Men and Other Poems,* 1907

---

[37] Ibid.

By May 1855, the two sides were ready to move their battle to the courthouse in Houma. Each had been afforded more than enough time to refine their respective strategies. From the outset of the legal proceedings, opposing attorneys focused the testimony of friendly witnesses on advancing their side's narrative. [38] The cross-examinations, however, were anything but friendly. The exchanges were, more often than not, long, grueling affairs.

Early in the proceedings, the Voisin camp decided that since attorney F. C. Laville was the originator of the map of Isle Longue that was to be central to its arguments, he [Laville] would relinquish his role as lead counsel so that he too could testify about the controversy and, perhaps more importantly, his 1851 map of Isle Longue. For their part, Wafford's attorneys determined to focus their cross-examinations on undercutting the credibility of Voisin's witnesses.

G. F. Connelly was unusually aggressive in his attacks on the memories of the old fishermen and seamen.

"What was the population of New Orleans during the year 1803?"

"Was the fish trade of New Orleans very important at that time and were men in the habit of coming so far west as Last Island in order to supply...New Orleans with fish?"

"For what length of time to your personal knowledge did Jean Voisin Sr. and Jr. reside continuously on...[Isle Longue]?"

"What kind of house did he occupy?"

"How much land did he cultivate and what kind of crops did he have?"

"Where did Jean Voisin Jr. reside in 1835?" [39]

The first to testify on behalf of Jean Joseph Voisin was Jerome Moreno of New Orlean. The old seaman, who had been born in Italy, described himself, in the simplest of terms, as *"now a gardener, formerly...a sailor."* [40] Voisin attorney Miles Taylor began by asking Moreno to explain how he knew of Jean Voisin and Isle Longue. Moreno's answer took those in the courtroom back to the year 1820.

"I have visited it frequently in passing by on my way to the Sabine [River] [41] and back...This island was called also 'Isle a Voisin' and it took its name from Mr. Voisin who lived on it."

---

[38] At the beginning of 1855, Jean Joseph Voisin was represented by attorneys Charles Maurian and Miles Taylor III; James Wafford's were represented by attorneys G. F. Connelly and Abram F. Rightor.

[39] *Public Land Claims, Number 4533*, National Archives and Records Administration, Washington DC.

[40] Ibid.

[41] The Sabine River is approximately 180 miles west of Last Island. The river forms the border between Louisiana and Texas.

"I know an island, which is called Last Island, and also an island called Wine Island. Last Island is situated on the north of Isle Longue…Wine Island is to the east of Isle Longue. Last Island was separated from Isle Longue by a bayou, which was called Bayou Voisin. In high water there were from three to four feet of water on it and was about half an acre in breadth. I have passed through this bayou in a small boat…" [42]

Attorney Taylor spread a large, over-sized cloth map in front of Moreno and asked the old man to identify several landmarks, each of which had been annotated with a letter from the alphabet.[43]

"I have examined the sketch…and recognize it as a correct representation…..Isle Longue was from twenty-one to twenty-two miles long…varying in widths…[from Raccoon Point] to the letter X on the sketch,[is] about six to seven miles of high and firm land, the balance of the island was low and marshy ground…Last Island was a low marshy soil…"

When asked by what name or names the coastal waters west of the Mississippi River were called, Moreno explained that *"the seaboard bordering on that part of Louisiana was…generally known by the name of Bay of Barataria or Lake Barataria…Isle Longue, and Timbalier Island were considered as being in Bay Barataria."* [44]

The attorney turned his witness' attention to the map of Isle Longue and Last Island and asked him to locate the Voisins' home. Moreno pointed to an "X" marked on the map and then noted that *"the position of Voisin's home is correctly marked…It was opposite the Bayou Voisin entrance."* [45]

During cross-examination, Wafford's attorneys repeatedly impugned the motives and credibility of Moreno. Connelly pressed hard to prove that Moreno lacked the skills and knowledge necessary to make such detailed observations. The old seaman, though, steadfastly held his ground.

"I am in no manner related to the defendant…Mr. Voisin asked me to come and give my testimony but neither he nor anyone has ever spoke to me of the nature of testimony I was to give…The facts that I state are from personal observations."

"The depth of water, I know from having used my pole when navigating through; the length of Isle Longue, I presume from the time it took me to walk from one end of it to the other…from observation. I never used any instruments."

"I am not a surveyor. I am a sailor."

---

[42] *Public Land Claims, Number 4533*, National Archives and Records Administration, Washington DC.

[43] The map used during court proceedings was the map of Isle Longue and Last Island, which F. C. Laville had created in 1851. The map contained numerous alphabetical annotations, each signifying a relevant landmark. The original cloth map and three copies are presently in the possession of the National Archives and Records Administration in Washington DC.

[44] *Public Land Claims, Number 4533*, National Archives and Records Administration, Washington DC.

[45] Ibid.

31

Next to testify on behalf of Voisin was thirty year-old oysterman and seafarer Pierre Bromen. A former pilot on the steamer *Fuselier*, Bromen demonstrated an equally impressive knowledge of Louisiana's coastal waters.

"I am licensed by the government to run that coast. I became acquainted with these islands by often frequenting them every summer for the last fifteen….I know an island heretofore commonly called Isle Longue, but now designated as 'Last Island.'" I have…visited this island…at least a thousand times for fishing, hunting and for the purpose of finding the channel…"

"This island was also called Voisin Island…[it] was commonly called by that name, by all the navigators along that coast." [46]

Echoing Moreno's testimony, Bromen recalled that Last Island and Isle Longue were separated by Voisin's Bayou.

"Last Island was to the north of Isle Longue…[the bayou] was about two feet deep and in some parts, it was 6-8 feet deep. It was from 125 to 200 feet wide. I have passed through in on boats in 1837. This bayou on the west end is filled up…it began to fill up in 1838 and I could not get through on my sailboat…Last Island was a low marshy island…it was then and is now covered by a high tide. It was from three to six miles long and very narrow." [47]

"Isle Longue lies to the west of …El Vino [Wine Island]…[and] was about twenty to twenty-three miles long…it is irregular in its breadth…I cannot say how much firm and high land there was…The low lands were and are still covered by water at times on the line marked on the plan from B and C, the high land principally laid at the point marked X there is a hill called Casolacer Camp, and at the place marked D, there is a little grove of trees called Musgento Grove; the balance of the island is all low." [48]

Voisin's attorney asked Bromen to explain how Isle Longue could be considered to have been situated in Lake Barataria or Bay Barataria.

"The sea bordering on the parishes of Jefferson, Lafourche and Terrebonne was generally known by the name of Lake Barataria or Bay Barataria by old navigators. I cannot say when it has ceased to be called by that name." [49]

The old seaman told the court how he knew of the Voisins and their fishing enterprise on the island.

---

[46] Ibid.

[47] Ibid.

[48] Much of the testimony involved the map F. C. Laville had made during the summer of 1851. He had annotated the map with several letters to mark the location of certain landmarks. The numerous references to "B. C…D and X" were markings on the map used in the courtroom.

[49] *Public Land Claims, Number 4533*, National Archives and Records Administration, Washington DC.

"I know Mr. Voisin…he was frequently pointed out to me…I saw him but a few times…He built himself a pretty good house, known as Voisin's Camp and had all the fixings around it necessary for a fisherman. He was fishing, hunting and much a considerable quantity of them [was] to send to the New Orleans market. I was not in the habit of visiting him, although I went frequently to the island."

"I know intimately…Mr. Jean Voisin, the son of Voisin Sr. I have known him for the last 15 years in the parish of Plaquemines and on Isle Longue. He resides now on Isle Longue near his father's camp." [50]

Bromen was asked if another island named Isle Longue may have once existed.

"There is no other island along the…coast known by the name Isle Longue…sometimes and but recently Grand Isle has been called by the name of Isle Longue, but this is wrong and it is not recognized as such." [51]

In an effort to preempt attacks by Wafford's attorneys on the motives of the witness, Bromen was asked to explain why he was in court.

"I am not related to the defendant…Mr. Voisin called upon me in the boat and requested me to call at the Justice's office for the purpose of giving my testimony as to my knowledge of the coasts, but did not instruct me to the nature of my evidence." [52]

When they took their turn, Wafford's attorneys wasted little time in attacking Bromen. Assailing the witness with the same ferocity directed at Moreno, the attorneys challenged Bromen to explain how such an uneducated seaman could accurately measure distances and areas. The weathered steamboat pilot was unflappable.

"I never made any measurements by instruments. I have often taken soundings with a pole and my lead piece, inside and outside of the islands. I was a pilot on the Steamship Fusilier and have been thus employed on several other boats. I am not a surveyor, but I am a navigator by long practice and know the whole coast from Southwest Pass to the mouth of the Rio Grande." [53]

As they would do throughout the proceedings, Wafford's attorneys asked Bromen to talk about Lake Barataria.

"I have heard it called Bay Barataria by Captain Allen, Pierre Tivet and Ganna and by others…They were fishermen and pirates living in that neighborhood…I had bought fish (dried red) and turtles for Tivet's from Voisin's Island to New Orleans."

---

[50] Ibid.

[51] Grand Isle was for a brief period referred to as "*Long Island*," a name reflected on an 1838 map of Louisiana by cartographer Thomas Bradford. This designation, however, was short-lived.

[52] Ibid.

[53] Ibid.

Bromen was asked to describe Jean Joseph Voisin's property holdings.

"As to what property he has, I believe he owns nothing but his household furniture and his claim to the land in dispute. I have known him for about 15 years…He lived somewhere near Pointe a la Hache [but has]…resided on Isle Longue for the last eight." [54]

Two days later, on May 3, 1855, Jean Baptiste Benate of New Orleans testified that he too was intimate with every aspect of the Louisiana coastline west of the Southwest Pass to the Mississippi River. Benate attributed his knowledge of the coast to his many visits there from 1811 through about 1825. Although he had not traveled to the islands during the past thirty years, Benate's recall was unambiguous.

"I know an island called Isle Longue, I went there to take permissions to Mr. Voisin, the father of the present defendant, who lived on the island."

"I was acquainted with Mr. Jean Voisin, the senior. He did reside on Isle Longue, I saw him there in 1812, 1813 and 1814. He was a fisherman, catching redfish and turtles. The redfish he dried and sent with the turtles to New Orleans. He had built himself a wooden house and fixed up the neighborhood for his fishing apparatus. He had also a small garden with vegetables, raised fowls and pigs." [55]

Benate recalled that Voisin had a partner – a Pierre Dinet - who *"followed the same business as Voisin, they caught, dried redfish and caught turtles, for the New Orleans markets."* [56]

Next to testify on behalf of Jean Joseph Voisin was a seventy-year-old tinsmith from New Orleans - Jean Pierre Catour. Following the lead of the other witnesses, Catour exhibited a thorough knowledge of the Louisiana coast, particularly the one hundred and twenty miles stretch the Southwest Pass to the Mississippi River and Pointe au Fer to the west at the discharge of the Atchafalaya River.

Catour testified that he first visited Louisiana's westernmost islands in 1811 and returned the following year with American troops at the onset of the War of 1812. Catour acknowledged that he was much more familiar with the waters around Grand Terre and Grand Isle but added that he also sailed in the waters to the west.

"I knew it [Isle Longue] for the first time in 1811 and ever since that time, I first knew it, by going there with Mr. Pierre Dinet, the partner of Mr. Jean Voisin, Sr. to fish with them. I know some of the islands along that coast. I am acquainted with isle a Vine, Cat Island, Isle Longue and a little [island] alongside of Isle Longue, the name of which I do not remember, nor can I state the bearings of the islands." [57]

---

[54] Ibid.

[55] Ibid.

[56] Ibid.

[57] Ibid.

34

When challenged, Catour explained the basis of his knowledge.

"I...became acquainted with it [Isle Longue] in 1811. I went there several times. It was three days at a time and I went out fishing with Mr. Dinet and Mr. Voisin, Sr. This island also called L'Isle au Voisin"...took its name from Mr. Voisin. Isle Longue was sometimes called Last Island." [58]

Catour was pressed regarding his assertion that there was a small island adjacent to Isle Longue.

"The little island [was] separated by a bayou from Isle Longue. I do not remember how it was called. The bayou was known as Bayou Voisin. There were five or six feet of water...I cannot say how broad it was.I passed through this bayou on an oyster boat in the years 1811 or 1812."

"This little island was on one end of Isle Longue and Mr. Voisin's house and toward the main shore. It was a flat island. As far as I remember, the island was about two arpents[59] wide in some places and the ground was high where Mr. Voisin had his house..." [60]

As always, the questioning invariably returned to the matter of Lake Barataria. Were the waters around Last Island and Wine Island ever referred to as such?

"Yes, it was known as Barataria Bay or Lake as far back, as I can remember Isle Longue was in Lake Barataria. This coast was designated as Barataria. It has been called so, as long as I can remember. I would apply that description to Isle Longue."

"I cannot say how many years [Voisin] lived there. He had built a wooden cabin and fixed up the things for his trade had a little patch where he raised some vegetables, and he was a fisherman, dried his redfish and sent turtles to market..." [61]

Voisin's attorney asked Catour if there could there have been another island called Isle Longue.

"I know of no other Isle Longue or of any other El Vino island, than those spoken of."

During cross-examination, Wafford's attorney challenged Catour's knowledge of the Terrebonne and Lafourche parish coastlines. How was the witness able to make such convincing judgments regarding the sizes of islands and the depth and width of the bayou?

"I have described the islands I know, but cannot say which are opposite the coasts of Terrebonne or Lafourche...I know it [Isle Longue] only by name. I made no measurements, sounded the bayou with my pole and no instruments."

Wafford's attorney asked Catour's to explain how he came to know Jean Joseph Voisin.

---

[58] Ibid.

[59] A linear arpent is approximately 192 feet.

[60] *Public Land Claims, Number 4533*, National Archives and Records Administration, Washington DC.

[61] Ibid.

"I have known J. Voisin, Jr. from his early youth. In 1835, he lived at Pointe á la Hache…I cannot say how long he has resided on Isle Longue." [62]

One line of questioning proved to be most curious. Voisin's attorney Charles Maurian asked several of his witnesses to describe what one had called a most *"remarkable tree."*

Pierre Bromen remembered that Last Island had *"a Hackberry tree on it - a Bois Canne or Canna."* [63] The tree was significant to Jerome Moreno because he used it to gauge distances and directions.

"The distance from the point on the sketch marked as Voisin's settlement to El Vino is about eighteen mile…in fair weather from the top of Bois Conner it can be seen with the naked eye."

Jean Baptiste Benate used the tree as a way of distinguishing one island from the other.

"I know there was a small island on the north of Isle Longue, separated from it by a bayou; on the small island there was a remarkable tree, which served as a signal stick, but I do not remember the name." [64]

Before court adjourned, Voisin's attorneys placed two additional affidavits into evidence. One was a sworn statement by Lange Lanata, a well-known merchant from New Orleans, the other an affidavit sworn to by a sixty-six year-old fisherman and hunter - Jacques Terrebonne.

Lanata testified that he too was *"…acquainted with Jean Voisin on Long Island, now called Last Island, west of Wine Island, in 1812. At that time a bayou carved out part of the island into a smaller portion then called Last Island."* For his part, Jacques Terrebonne stated that he was first *"…acquainted with Jean Voisin in 1802 on what was then known as Long Island, west of Wine Island, but is currently called Last Island…"* [65]

Terrebonne claimed to possess firsthand knowledge of every island west of the Mississippi River. In particular, he was familiar with Isle Longue and Wine Island and had never heard of another island in the region named Wine Island. Terrebonne, who had visited Isle Longue at least ten times, noted that in earlier days Timbalier Bay was known as Lake Barataria.

Jacques Terrebonne observed that Isle Longue was under water much of the time. He recalled that the only reliable high ground on Isle Longue was a five or six-mile stretch on the western end. It was on that part of the island that the elder Voisin had built his house. It was in that location on the island that the elder Voisin maintained a vegetable garden, gathered wax and caught fish and sea turtles for the New Orleans market. Echoing other witnesses, Terrebonne

---

[62] Ibid.

[63] Bromen seems to have been referring to the *Bois Canot* or *Trumpet Tree*, which is a fast-growing, deciduous tree found in tropical regions. The *Bois Canot*, which has large palmate leaves can grow to twenty-five meters in height.

[64] *Public Land Claims, Number 4533*, National Archives and Records Administration, Washington DC.

[65] Ibid.

described the narrow bayou that separated the smaller *Derniere Isle* from Isle Longue.

Former lead counsel F. C. Laville was one of the last witnesses called by Voisin's attorneys. His appearance was delayed as a way of reinforcing the importance and relevance of the Isle Longue map, which had been referenced time and time again by Voisin's witnesses. When Connelly finally got his chance to challenge the map's creator, he attacked with a vengeance.

Laville, though, patiently parried each thrust, first describing the invitation he had received from Voisin to spend the summer of 1851 on Isle Longue. For two months, Laville walked and sailed about the island, methodically sketching all that he observed. Laville acknowledged that he had annotated the map with letters of the alphabet as a way of identifying key landmarks.

The map markings were used repeatedly to distinguish the "high and firm" west end from the "*low and marshy*" land masses. Laville responded calmly to each and every Connelly attempt to discredit him.

"Are you or have you ever been a Civil Engineer, surveyor or navigator or have you ever practiced either profession; are you a practical geologist?"

"Supposing the bayou which you call Bayou Voisin has been filled up, for what distance has it been filled up?"

"If there is any [land] accretion or aggression [66]*...indicating the bed of the old bayou...what is the depth of such aggression?"*

"Are you accustomed to surveying or measuring distances or to the use of surveying and nautical instruments?"

"Have you had any experience in topographical plats or plans? What kind of instruments did you use...?" [67]

"I have never studied the tides and currents of the ocean...never paid any particular attention to the operation of tides and currents on forming deposits. I made this sketch [of Isle Longue and Last Island] more with a view of information and ascertaining the localities than with a view of absolute accuracy." [68]

Laville explained that that he had charted and measured the bayou – labeled on his map as "*Bayou Voisin*" - with a sea compass as he navigated about the two islands in a skiff. He explained that his estimates of distances were based on familiar landmarks and a general sense of how far one was from the other.

Laville's testimony returned with regularity to the significance of the bayou – a waterway that

---

[66] Connelly's references to coastal "*aggression*" pertained to coastal or land erosion.

[67] *Public Land Claims, Number 4533*, National Archives and Records Administration, Washington DC.

[68] Ibid.

began on the north side about six miles from the westernmost tip of the island. The bayou cut into the island for a short distance and then angled sharply to the west, reconnecting again with Caillou Bay, less than one-half mile from Raccoon Point. Laville's map depicted a bayou that followed a semi-circular route that divided the two land masses, creating a small island on the northwest side of Isle Longue, an island Voisin and others identified as Last Island.

When challenged by Connelly about the existence of two islands, Laville was forced to acknowledge that more recently the extreme western portion of the bayou had filled in, reconnecting the two islands. Connelly listened intently and then ridiculed any notion that there had ever been two distinct and separate islands.

Connelly demanded that his adversary explain the disappearance of the bayou's western extent. How could such a body of water disappear? Laville explained that even in 1851, when he and Voisin passed through the bayou in their skiff, they found that, as they approached Raccoon Point, the bayou "*diminished to the size of a ditch.*"

By 1854 or 1855, Laville's "*ditch*" near the western end of the islands had had completely dried, reconnecting the two land masses. Shifting gears, Connelly returned once again to the question of Laville's involvement in the case.

"*Are not the attorneys employed in this case to receive a portion of the property recovered? Was not your visit to Last Island more for the purpose of getting a case?*"

Laville rejected Connelly's final accusation that there was some nefarious contingency arrangement involved. He reminded Wafford's attorney that Voisin had since engaged attorneys Charles Maurian and the Taylors to serve as legal counsel. Laville did acknowledge that St. Mary Parish planter George Haydel, a supporter of Voisin, had suggested some alternate form of compensation for in the event Voisin was unable to pay Laville for his effort but that only because Voisin had such limited resources.

The witnesses for Jean Joseph Voisin had said their piece. They were simple men from south Louisiana – fishermen, seamen and artisans. It was now time to hear from those who would challenge the claims of Jean Joseph Voisin. It was time to hear from those who would support the claims of James Nixon Wafford – it was time for the kings to step forth.

Chapter Six: ...and Kings

"That this and the rest of what hath hitherto been spok'n is most true, might be copiously made appear throughout all Stories Heathen and Christian; ev'n of

*those Nations where Kings and Emperours have sought meanes to abolish all
ancient memory of the Peoples right by thir encroachments and usurpations."*
- John Milton, from *The Tenure of Kings and Magistrates* (1650)

In filing suit against Jean Joseph Voisin, thirty-eight year-old James Wafford of Franklin
assumed the role of principle protagonist in the protracted contest over who really owned Last
Island. The witnesses who were asked to testify on behalf of Wafford personified images of
staggering wealth, power, privilege and confidence. Within the social circles of antebellum
Louisiana, James Wafford and his Last Island neighbors were undeniably the elite within the
elite. How could Jean Joseph Voisin, a simple, solitary fisherman, hope to contend with such an
assemblage?

The Wafford camp wasted little time. Before the first witness testified, three Wafford supporters
joined together and penned a letter to the State Land Office. The text contained in the letter was
a thinly disguised rehearsal for the looming court case. Signing the letter were three St. Mary
Parish planters - Elias Beers, Pinckney C. Bethel and Thomas Maskell. Each man possessed a
certificate of purchase issued by the State Land Office for a tract of land on Last Island. They
got right to the point.

*"The undersigned residents of the parish of St. Mary respectfully represent that they are the
owners by purchase from the United States of certain tracts of land situated on Last or Derniere
Island in the parish of Terrebonne in Township 24, Range 15 East, Southeastern district of
Louisiana."* [69]

Continuing their well-honed narrative, they characterized the claims of Jean Joseph Voisin as
fraudulent and illegitimate.

*"The undersigned deny that…Voisin has any title or valid claim to any portion of the lands…the
tract confirmed to Jean Voisin is a 'small island situated in the Lake of Barataria, Parish of
Jefferson and commonly called L'isle Longue containing 600 superficial arpents and fronting on
one side another small island called El Vino.'"*

*"The land claimed by the undersigned is situated upon Last Island fronting on the Gulf of
Mexico in the parish of Terrebonne and at a distance of at least 70 miles from the Lake of
Barataria and so far from being a small island is more that twenty miles long and containing
about 10,000 acres."*

Beers, Bethel and Maskell insisted that Last Island *"has never been known as L'Isle Longue or
Voisin's Island."* They smugly reasoned that this could not have been the case because, as
everyone knew, Voisin's island was *"situated at or near Barataria Bay in the parish of
Jefferson."*

Maskell and his friends reminded the State Register and Receiver that the Louisiana Surveyor

---

[69] *Public Land Claims, Number 4533*, National Archives and Records Administration, Washington DC.

General had never surveyed nor located an island called Isle Longue. That fact alone meant that the State Land Office had *"no right"* to fix the location of Isle Longue on Last Island. The final paragraph of the letter was meant to preempt assertions being made by Voisin's attorneys that both Last Island and Isle Longue had undergone dramatic topographical changes over the past sixty years. This was an indirect but clear reference to the map attorney F. C. Laville was planning to enter into evidence.

"[We] object to any testimony…[that shows] great changes in the topography…by which Last Island is made to appear…a small island on one side of the land claimed by the undersigned as Last Island…"

Thomas Maskell followed the trio's letter with an equally impassioned personal appeal to the Commissioner of the General Land Office in Washington – John Wilson. Maskell charged that Jean Joseph Voisin was falsely claiming land that he [Maskell] had *"purchased from the United States Government on good faith, and on which I have erected valuable improvements…all of which…I have by patent granted in good faith."*

Mirroring the first missive, Maskell sought to undercut any influence the Laville map might have in court. His letter to Wilson focused on what he characterized as critical discrepancies between the 1851 sketch by Laville and the Surveyor General's official 1838 Last Island survey plats.

"The diagram filed [the Laville map]*…is not correct as you can see by reference to the survey lately made by the surveying department of the United States…[in addition] Voisin's first petition does not claim the land and his grant must be confined to his petition."*[70]

On October 2, 1855, attorneys for James Wafford called the first in a long procession of prominent witnesses - sixty-seven year-old Adolphe Labauve. The highly respected planter from St. Mary Parish testified that he first visited the island in 1814. Connelly asked Labauve if he had ever noted during this forty-year period any significant topographical changes to the island.

"[I] do not know of any changes…[during] my visit, I went to a bayou that ran up into the island the mouth of which I should think now which began [to] form the west end of the island."[71]

Connelly pressed Labauve for a detailed description of the bayou. Did the bayou pass all the way through the island and exit again on the Gulf? Or, did it enter on the Caillou Bay side, turn to the west and reconnect with Caillou Bay to the west, as depicted on Laville's map?

"[The] bayou…when I saw it did not communicate with the sea or with the bay excepting by the mouth were I landed…"

By what name did Labauve know the island?

"[I] never heard the island above described nor any other island in that vicinity called Isle

---

[70] Ibid.

[71] Ibid.

Longue, if said island had been formerly known as Isle Longue…[I] would have heard it."

Labauve recalled the presence of only one man on the island – a Fifi Garcia, who was living on the island with his son at the time of his visit.

"[Garcia] was employed in piloting Lafitte's vessels around the west end of the island into the Bay Caillou…[he] lived in a small camp at the mouth of the bayou…[I have] no evidence of any [other] habitation on the island…"

As he had done with Voisin's witnesses, Connelly asked Labauve if he had ever heard the waters around Last Island referred to as Lake Barataria.

"[I] never heard the waters around Last Island called Barataria Bay…and think such waters never could have been so designated without my knowing it."

Thomas Jones was the next witness to speak in support of James Wafford. The fifty year-old sugar planter from St. Mary Parish had lived in Franklin for more than thirty years.

"I know a place called Last Island, first visited it nearly 30 years ago…the length of the island was nearly equal then to what it is now, the sea in high tides and heavy blows occasionally washed over the island toward the east end."

"I visited the island almost every year generally in the winter…[I] know of no great changes in the appearance or extent of the island since I first knew it." [72]

Connelly directed Jones' attention to the bayou.

"I am acquainted with a bayou that leads in the island at about a mile from the west end and communicates with Caillou Bay at about two miles and a half from the west end, never knew said bayou to run through to the sea, so as to cut Last Island into two islands. I have never heard the place above described as Last Island could have been formerly known as Isle Longue…"

Had Jones ever seen Jean Joseph Voisin or his father on Last Island?

"There were no inhabitants on Last Island when I first knew it…no indication to show that the island has ever been inhabited, excepting a pile of oyster shells. I never knew or heard of Jean Voisin, Sr. I know a man named Jean Voisin, now living on the island, have known him as a resident of Last Island for about 7 years." [73]

Connelly continued his refrain, asking Jones if he had ever heard the waters around Last Island referred to as Lake Barataria or Barataria Bay. Jones pondered the question and said that, as far as he knew, the waters between Last Island and the Terrebonne Parish coastline were known as Caillou Bay and Lake Pelto.

---

[72] *Public Land Claims, Number 4533*, National Archives and Records Administration, Washington DC.
[73] Ibid.

41

By far, the most influential witness was former United States Congressman John Moore. James Wafford could not have hoped for a more towering courtroom presence. A powerful planter-politician, Moore represented the State of Louisiana in the United States House of Representatives from 1840 to 1843 and again from 1851 to 1853. The former legislator divided his time between the plantation he and his wife Mary Conrad Weeks Moore shared in New Iberia – *Shadows on the Teche* – and a second, in St. Martin Parish. Few men in antebellum Louisiana were as wealthy, as well known or as powerful as sixty-seven year-old John Moore. He was a man the citizens of Louisiana listened to with deference.

"I know a place called Last Island, well I have been on it several times between the years 1834 and 1839 on fishing and hunting excursions...There was no settlement or vestige of settlement thereon in 1839. I found a [fishing] hut...[maintained] by Jose Matte, a fisherman for his own commission. I never heard of there being any settlement on it previous to 1839."

"I first saw Derniere Isle in June 1828. I was taking a small steamboat from the Teche, passed through Bayou Lafourche to the Mississippi River. I employed a pilot to show the way, 'Fifi' Gauche...who told me that he had often been along there when a boy with his father, he pointed out and names the places as we went along, we went through Oyster Bayou...north of Last Island, which he pointed out as Derniere Isle, we continued along on the north or inside of Last Island [to] Wine Island...Fifi Gauche [74] *died several years ago."*

"I never heard him say that Last Island had been inhabited there, he seemed proud of his knowledge of that part of the country."

Turning once again to a familiar question, Connelly asked Moore to describe the bayou.

"I was acquainted with a bayou, which takes its rise near the west end of Last Island and falls into Oyster Bay generally called Caillou Bay, on the north side of Last Island, three or four miles from the west end...when I first visited...there were no appearances that said bayou ran through to the Bay or sea, near the east end so as to...[divide] Last Island into two islands...I do not believe that such a connection ever existed."

The witness was asked if the island had ever been called Isle Longue.

"I never heard...Last Island called Isle Longue until some such pretensions have been set up [during] the last five years...if it had ever been so called, I should have heard it."

Connelly then turned Moore's attention to Jean Joseph Voisin.

"I first became acquainted with Jean Voisin when my testimony was taken before the Register and Receiver last winter...[I] never heard that any person of that name had ever inhabited Last Island previous to my first visit...when I came to this country I did not hear that the island was

---

[74] *"Fifi Gauche"* and *"Fifi Garcia"* almost certainly refer to the same individual. Given the fact that there is a Bayou Fifi and a Bayou Gauche near Grand Isle suggests that Gauche, not Garcia, is the correct surname.

inhabited nor do I believe it."

Connelly concluded by asking Moore to explain the meaning of the term *"Lake Barataria."*

"I do not believe that the name of Barataria could have been given to these waters without my having heard it…I have now before me a map…on which Barataria Bay [or] Lac Barataria is laid down about four leagues east of [Bayou] Lafourche…[near] Grande Terre." [75]

Although, not a witness *per se*, Connelly cleverly found a way to testify indirectly by asking witnesses to comment on correspondence and maps that he had himself authored. One letter had been written by Connelly to the State Register. Witnesses cited that in the letter, Connelly had suggested that by virtue of his client's 1848 purchase of land from the United States, James Wafford was the legitimate owner of the contested 53-acre tract of land on Last Island.

"[Wafford] has a full and perfect title to the same from the United States…[and] denies that Voisin has any claim on said island or that if he has, that said claim has never been located and that this office, or this court, has no right to locate and fix the same." [76]

Connelly reminded the court that the official survey of Last Island had been under the *"control and direction"* of the United States surveying department for more than ten years.

"The Surveyor General of the United States for the State of Louisiana having refused to locate the claim of Voisin on [Last Island]…the whole matter becomes a question of title for the consideration of the courts of the country and this office has no jurisdiction…"

The procession of witnesses testifying against Jean Joseph Voisin was complete. With the 1855 court calendar winding down, opposing sides increasingly realized that the mirroring cases of *Wafford versus Voisin* and *Voisin versus Wafford et al* had morphed into a curious cacophony of chaos, confusion and contradiction. Each side was more than eager for the upcoming winter hiatus. On that note, the presiding judge for the Fifth District Court in Terrebonne Parish advised the attorneys in November that the case would resume *"next year."*

Next year, of course, was 1856.

If the court docket in Houma was anything like the preceding years, the legal combatants might have just enough time for a brief respite before returning to the courthouse. By June, the cooling waters and refreshing breezes of the Gulf and the smooth white beaches of Last Island would be calling. Hundreds would heed that call. They did so oblivious to the fact that for most – and for Last Island itself – the summer of 1856 would be their last days.

Chapter Seven: August 1856 – A Great Storm, an Island Lost

Weep for the living! For the dead rest 'neath the briny deep – Kissed by the dark sea's silvery spray, in quietness they sleep. The angry wall that speaks

---

[75] *Public Land Claims, Number 4533*, National Archives and Records Administration, Washington DC.

[76] *Public Land Claims, Number 4533*, National Archives and Records Administration, Washington DC.

above the tempest's fearful rave, harms not the dead who lie entombed beneath the ocean's wave! - Dr. W. B. Wood, from *Weep for the Living*, a poem published in the New Orleans *Daily Picayune*, September 6, 1856

The denizens of south Louisiana greeted the summer of 1856 with a shimmering optimism. The sugar economy was flourishing and thoughts of the yellow fever epidemic in New Orleans, which claimed upwards of 13,000 victims in 1853, had finally waned. The clouds of civil war, though looming, were still distant enough to disregard. It was that time of year during which antebellum Louisiana turned its thoughts to Last Island - summer was at hand.

The legal lethargy that defined the competing civil suits between James Wafford and Jean Joseph Voisin was a poor match for the excitement generated by the weekly pilgrimages to Last Island. Throughout the southeastern parishes, wealthy planters, powerful politicians and influential merchants gathered together their families, neighbors and slaves and departed for the island, eager to settle into fashionable seaside homes, the Muggahs' sprawling hotel or one of its several adjacent cottages.

Thibodaux's Mary Anne Scofield Beausergeant, though, was an exception to the euphoria of the moment. Her days were filled with thoughts of an upcoming court appearance in the Fifth District Court in Houma. The sixty-six year-old widow of Jean Baptiste Beausergeant had been subpoenaed to testify on behalf of James Wafford in the ongoing land dispute. Wafford attorney G. F. Connelly was poised with his familiar set of questions.

"How long have you known said island?"

"What name or names has the said island been called and known by ever since you first knew or heard of it?"

"Has Last Island undergone any change since you first knew it, if so please state in what that change consisted and particularly whether there have been any and what changes in the western or northwestern part of the island?"

"Was there ever a bayou flowing through any part of said island so as to form two islands, instead of one?"

"Was any portion of Last Island settled on and occupied previous to 1840?" [77]

If Connelly's questions had a familiar ring, so too did Beausergeant's answers.

Mary Anne Beausergeant had lived in Thibodaux since the early 1840s. When her husband died in 1843, she turned the family home into a boarding house. The widow Beausergeant was well acquainted with the dispute's principal protagonists - James Wafford and Jean Joseph Voisin. Carefully considering every Connelly question, she answered each with an air of certainty.

---

[77] *Public Land Claims, Number 4533*, National Archives and Records Administration, Washington DC.

"I know an island called Last Island...it is situated in t he parish of Terrebonne...twenty-eight miles long on...[to] the east lies Wine Island to the west Racoon [Point]... in some places it is a mile across in others two."

Connelly asked if she had ever heard the island called anything other than Derniere Isle or Last Island.

"The island has always been called Derniere Isle, ever since I knew it or heard of it. It was always called so by others."

Beausergeant said that she had *"never heard it called by the name of Long Island..."* and then added derisively *"...until Mr. Voisin called it so, in my presence and I laughed."* Connelly asked Beausergeant if she had noticed any changes in the island's topography during the past fifteen years.

"Yes...it has grown larger, in some places...decreased in others. The western part...has been cut off a good deal...[I have never known of] a bayou flowing through any part of this island."

Beausergeant's final response confirmed that she knew of no one actually living on the island before 1840. She was only aware of the presence of an occasional fishing camp.

"One quarter of a mile from the Muggah Hotel, eastward was a fishery called Carlos' Camp. This is all I know." [78]

Prior to the beginning of 1856 court session in Houma, attorneys for Jean Joseph Voisin expanded their suit against Wafford to include several other defendants - David R. Muggah, Alexander Field, Pinkney C. Bethel and others.

The slow-moving trial in Houma, though, was about to be upstaged. Miles to the east, a large swirling cloud formation was moving slowly through the Gulf of Mexico. By the first week in August, the massive, counter-clockwise menace was inching its way toward Louisiana's central coast. Squarely in its path was *Isle Derniere* – Last Island.

Nearly four hundred south Louisianans had gathered on the island, desiring only to swap the long hot days of summer for a few weeks of leisure. By mid-afternoon on Sunday, August 10th, the storm's powerful winds, estimated by the National Oceanic and Atmospheric Administration (NOAA) to have reached 140 miles per hour[79], slammed ashore. The ravaging winds were followed by a nine-foot tidal surge. When Nature's work had been completed, the storm had flattened every structure on the island, drowned or crushed an estimated two hundred men, women and children. More than two hundred survivors were scattered indiscriminately about the

---

[78] Ibid.

[79] The National Hurricane Center (NHC) produced an analysis of the 1856 storm, which is in the *Atlantic Hurricane Database Re-analysis Project.* The NHC has reconstructed storms as far back as 1851. This is an ongoing project of the Hurricane Research Division, National Hurricane Center, National Oceanic and Atmospheric Administration (NOAA).

devastated island or washed across Caillou Bay into Terrebonne Parish's harsh coastal marshes.

To the south and east of the island, another one hundred and thirty men, women and children perished as their vessels capsized in the roiling waters of the Gulf of Mexico. By day's end, more than three hundred people were dead. Hundreds more were clinging desperately to life, scattered about the island, afloat on the waters of the Gulf or in the hostile environs of Terrebonne Parish's coastal marshes. For survivors, the desperate struggle to stay alive was just beginning.

Three days passed before communities on the mainland learned of the disaster. Two more days would pass before weary rescuers returned to the interior with the first survivors. Search parties continued to recover bodies for weeks following the storm. By week two, few of the bodies were even identifiable. Most were badly decomposed and, in the absence of some form of identifying jewelry or clothing, buried where they were found. Those victims that were identified were returned to the arms of grieving families.

What followed was a nightmare for the citizens of south Louisiana. Days of grueling, heart-rending efforts to rescue trapped survivors turned into weeks of combing through the scattered debris and miles of coastal marshes looking for bodies. Area newspapers did what they could to inform their readers of the devastation. More often than not, they published erroneous or conflicting lists of survivors and victims.

Dozens of names tied directly or indirectly to the legal proceedings involving Isle Longue and Last Island were found among the names on the published lists. Jean Joseph Voisin and his two sons survived the ordeal. Voisin's wife and nine year-old daughter, Jean Amelie and Marie Amelie, did not. Others involved in the litigation perished that day.

Thomas Maskell, his wife and two children; Michael Schlatre's wife and seven children; Antoine Comeau's wife and five children; Thomas Mille, his wife, son daughter-in-law and one grandchild; brothers John and James Muggah, and several members of their respective families; Joseph Achille Hebert, his wife and one child; and scores more. [80]

In the aftermath of the great storm, few cared about who may or may not have owned land on Last Island. The trauma and devastation of the August 10 storm had obliterated such pedestrian concerns. Still, in the midst of such complete and utter ruin, flotsam from the *Wafford versus Voisin* and *Voisin versus Wafford et al* continued to surface in the months to come.

Only weeks before the storm struck, attorneys for Voisin had attempted to obtain a statement from Louis St. Martin. St. Martin had been the State Register in 1848, the year in which Maskell and Wafford made the initial land purchases. Of interest to the attorneys was whether the former State Register had informed Maskell or Wafford of the protests of Jean Joseph Voisin. Louis St. Martin's deposition was received by the court in Houma shortly a few weeks after the disaster. St. Martin, who served as State Register from 1846 through 1849, acknowledged that he could not remember if, at the time of the initial purchases, he had advised Wafford and

---

[80] *Last Days of Last Island*, Bill Dixon, University of Louisiana at Lafayette Press (2009)

Maskell of Voisin's claims. He then volunteered his views on the merits of Voisin's case.

"As soon as I was acquainted with the title of Jean Voisin, I occasioned it well and became satisfied that he [Voisin] had a just title to the land in question."

St. Martin confessed that he faced a rather knotty professional predicament.

"I received no instructions to the best of my knowledge and belief concerning said claim. It is not the duty of the Register to locate claims. It is the Surveyor General's duty to do so. The land appeared as vacant on the Township Map and on the Tract Book. It was my imperative duty to sell it, even if I had been informed of the un-located claim of Voisin."

"If I had refused...I might have been liable for damages." [81]

Two months following the storm, a Fifth District Court judge in Houma reconvened the proceedings to consider a motion offered forth by James Wafford's attorneys. G. F. Connelly reminded the Court that many of the principals in the case were dead or still recovering from the effects of the storm. He asked that the judge continue the case. The motion was promptly accepted and on October 6, 1856, the two cases - *Wafford versus Voisin* and *Voisin versus Wafford et al* - were transferred to the October 1857 docket. [82]

In the months following the great storm, correspondence between the State Land Office and the General Land Office in Washington would surface, indicative of the snail-like movements of large, cumbersome bureaucracies. When the long overdue report of State Register Louis Palms and State Receiver H. W. Palfrey reached GLO Commissioner John Wilson, it was little more than a repackaging of testimony offered by former Congressman John Moore. The document merely echoed phrases from the earlier trial testimony.

Jean Joseph Voisin's property is but a *"small island containing about six hundred superficial arpents."*

"Last Island [which] is about twenty miles in length...certainly...can be no "small island" containing but 600 arpents!! The United States Surveys on file in this office show that the area exceeds eight thousand acres!...We are of opinion that Jean Voisin has failed to establish his claim to any part or portion of Last Island." [83]

Isle Longue is said to be situated in *"Lake of Barataria,"* not in the coastal waters of Terrebonne Parish. Barataria Bay, as everyone knows, *"...is an inland bay some sixty-five miles east of the island claimed and is in the parish of Jefferson."*

"Last Island is within the limits of the parish of Terrebonne [Parish]...It seems improbable to us, that Mr. Voisin or the person who acted as his agent could at that time have considered Last

[81] *Public Land Claims, Number 4533*, National Archives and Records Administration, Washington DC.
[82] Ibid.
[83] Ibid.

Island a 'small island' or its situation in the parish of Jefferson!!"

When Voisin attorney John Grymes learned of the Register and Receiver's report to the GLO, he fired off an equally impassioned letter to United States Senator John Slidell.

"This appears to be a very biased conclusion by Palms and Palfrey...This letter is full of half-truths and inferred conclusions, which are NOT proven by the testimony, it is clearly against Voisin."

"John Moore was in error in...his testimony where he states that no one resided on the island before 1828-1839. It must [be] noted at this time that just as today, there were many hurricanes and as was proven by the position of this island and the terrible disaster which took place in August 1856; we feel very sure that many times the houses of Jean Voisin and his business partner Pierre Dinet (de Nettei) were totally destroyed by the many storms and hurricanes." [84]

Such documents and letters moved back and forth between Louisiana and Washington throughout the spring and summer of 1857. By the time the October 1857 court calendar convened, counsel for both sides realized that post-storm circumstances were little changed. The parties central to the case were still scattered about the state, many still unable to travel to take part in the proceedings.

Opposing attorneys again asked the court for a continuance. The judge agreed, this time giving the parties a two-year respite. As had been the case in 1857, the two years changed little. By the time the 1859 court session convened, disinterest had replaced grieving and healing. Few cared about the land dispute any longer. On October 10, 1859, the judge listened to the motions of the two sides and granted yet another continuance. *Wafford versus Voisin* and *Voisin versus Wafford, Muggah, Field, Bethel, et al* would have to wait.

The two civil suits, along with the reams of testimony, evidence, motions and rulings, were filed away with the Terrebonne Parish Clerk of Court. The Fifth District Court and the citizens of Louisiana, it seems, now had more pressing matters on their minds. Another storm was brewing – one destined to quash for a generation all memories of Last Island and a increasingly unimportant land dispute.

On May 7, 1862, Judge Edward Simon convened his court one last time. He surveyed the room and then advised the opposing parties that all proceedings in the cases of *Wafford versus Voisin* and *Voisin versus Wafford et al* were suspended – indefinitely. The judge's decision was brief, his reasoning clear - *"The parish is being invaded by the North."*

"Court stands adjourned." [85]

With Civil War raging throughout the divided nation, any remaining interest in a stale, fourteen year-old land dispute understandably evaporated. On January 3, 1865, the Fifth District Court

---

[84] Ibid.

[85] Ibid.

received a cryptic note - Jean Joseph Voisin was not physically able to attend the court proceedings. It was a situation that was not likely to change. The Court excused Voisin and once again shelved the case – perhaps next year would be better.

When the scheduled October 1866 date arrived, it was evident that most of the principles in the case were dead, infirmed or in places unknown. There existed little reason to revisit the matter. To no one's surprise, the judge acted swiftly and mercifully. In November 1866, the Court transferred the cases of *Wafford versus Voisin* and *Voisin versus Wafford, Muggah, Field, Bethel, et al* to the Fifth District's *"dead docket."* [86]

Given the devastation of Civil War and the harsh days of Reconstruction, remaining memories of Last Island understandably faded from the State's collective consciousness. The story of August 10, 1856, lay dormant for more than thirty years. That, of course, changed in 1888, when renowned novelist Lafcadio Hearn resurrected the tragedy with publication of his masterpiece, *Chita: A Memory of Last Island.* But other than the exotic, hyperbolic images spawned by Hearn's classic work, little remained of Last Island. Even less remained of the bitter land disputed that had preceded the Great Storm of 1856.

Sixty-nine year-old Jean Joseph Voisin died in 1874 and was laid to rest. Also at rest on a shelf in the Terrebonne Parish courthouse was a box filled with an assortment of affidavits, maps and other documents that comprised the two civil suits. The bulky file that was *Wafford versus Voisin* and *Voisin versus Wafford et al* would remain there undisturbed for generations to come.

More than one hundred years later, knowledge of a litigious past – and of a rapidly disappearing barrier island – were far from the thoughts of the descendants of Jean Joseph Voisin. For one descendant - James Voisin - that was about to change.

The year was 1988.

Chapter Eight: A Slumbering Dispute Awakens

"In the heaviness of night, when all creatures seek the ghost of slumber, I sit up,

---

[86] Ibid.

singing at one time and sighing at another. I am awake always. Alas!
Sleeplessness has weakened me! But I am a lover, and the truth of love is strong. I
may weary, but I shall never die." – Kahlil Gibran, from *Song of the Wave* (1951)

In a span of only five years - from 1848 to 1853 - a small number of Louisiana sugar planters transformed a small, low-lying barrier island into the antebellum South's most fashionable watering spot – Last Island.   In a span of only five hours - from twelve noon to five o'clock on Sunday, August 10, 1856 - an unprecedented force of nature leveled the idyllic island village, returning it to what it had been when first granted to Jean Voisin in 1788 – a desolate spit of sand, good for little more than fishing, hunting and trapping.

In the decades following the great storm, fishermen and oystermen had unfettered access to Louisiana's eroding chain of barrier islands. That state of affairs, however, would not last indefinitely. Early in the 20th century, a Midwestern transplant from Michigan became interested in the coastal marshland that lay west of the Mississippi River.

Fascinated by the prospect of shoring up Louisiana's fragile marshes, Edward Wisner bought hundreds of thousands of acres. His goal was to reclaim Louisiana's low-lying marshlands by constructing an elaborate network of levees, similar to those constructed in the Netherlands to recapture its low-lying areas.

Wisner's plans for transforming the state's vast coastal region into fertile farmlands were short-lived. As always, the forces of nature had other plans. The most crippling blow was a September 29, 1915, hurricane, which slammed into south central Louisiana with one hundred and thirty mile-an-hour winds and a storm surge that topped ten feet.

The storm devastated Wisner's embryonic system of levees and his ambitious plans for the long term. Debt-ridden and facing the staggering prospect of bankruptcy, Wisner decided to sell much of his land to Henry Timken, a ball-bearing magnet from Ohio. Timken had dramatically different plans for south Louisiana's coastal marshlands. He intended to lease most of that acreage to hunters and fur trappers.

Timken's plans ran squarely into a much different reality - economics. Like Edward Wisner, he too was soon over-extended and, again like the man from Michigan, receptive to an intriguing proposition. In 1925, an Ohio speculator - Edward Simms - approached Timken and suggested that the two men join forces and form an oil exploration company. Simms and Timken negotiated for months before finally reaching an agreement in 1926. In the deal, Timken agreed to cede nearly 600,000 acres to Simms in exchange for shares in a newly formed company - the Border Research Corporation.

Executives in the company soon changed the name from the Border Research Company to Louisiana Land and Exploration (LL&E). It did not take long for the two businessmen to realize that they were sitting atop hundreds of thousands of petroleum-rich acres. In less than one year, LL&E leveraged that momentous fact. In 1927, Louisiana Land and Exploration signed an extraordinarily generous lease agreement with the Texas Company – Texaco.   Texaco was

50

eager to tap the deposits of oil and gas trapped beneath south Louisiana's numerous salt domes. The oil and gas behemoth made LL&E an offer it could not refuse. The two companies signed a contract that stipulated that Texaco would pay LL&E an unprecedented twenty-five percent royalty on all production and eight and one-third percent of net profits for each of its salt dome operations.

After a mutually enriching decade, the two companies modified their agreement in 1938. In the new deal, Texaco returned control of more than 500,000 acres to LL&E. Texaco retained only the acreage surrounding its vast salt dome operations. The return of so many acres opened the door to yet another fiscal boon for LL&E. The company was free to lease the reclaimed acreage to other oil and gas exploration companies.

Throughout the 1930s and 1940s, LL&E and its several oil and gas partners thrived financially. Louisiana Land and Exploration's uncanny ability to strike a deal, keyed the company's enormous financial success. Energy companies, desperate for access to Louisiana's oil and gas fields, were no match for LL&E negotiators.

The net result of the carefully crafted contracts was a long string of lease arrangements that were inordinately favorable to LL&E. Most of the agreements saddled the oil and gas companies with the expense of exploration and production, while leaving LL&E with few risks and incredible profits. In a 1965 *Dun's Review* interview, LL&E President Ford Graham boasted about the company's wildly successful business model.

"We pay twenty-five percent of the cost and get forty percent of the income. Texaco pays seventy-five percent and gets sixty. And they paid us a four million dollar bonus on the lease!"

The Louisiana Land and Exploration Corporation's staggeringly successful run was about to be interrupted. Buoyed by an air of invincibility, LL&E, like so many other *Fortune 500* conglomerates, succumbed to the lure of expansion. A fierce determination to expand and diversify proved to be LL&E's undoing.

With oil production in Louisiana on the decline, the company embarked on one ill-considered initiative after another. The economic turmoil of the 1970s, spawned by social and political upheaval in the Middle East and cemented by actions of the Organization of the Petroleum Exporting Countries (OPEC), served as a temporary respite for LL&E as the price of Louisiana oil spiked upwards for a while. That relief was short-lived.

Eventually, LL&E's precarious balancing act tipped in a direction that was adverse to the company's long term fiscal health. Strangled by a combination of industry economics, unpredictable demand for Louisiana oil, ill-conceived copper and real estate ventures, costly deep water drilling operations, high windfall-profit taxes, and increased federal and state regulation, LL&E's historical profit margins tumbled.

By the end of the 1980s, LL&E was forced to shed itself of its less profitable holdings. One opportunity to scale back its holdings came from an unexpected source – the federal government. Louisiana Land and Exploration had a long-standing and well-deserved reputation as a champion of Louisiana's delicate wetlands.[87]

Following the 1990 passage of the *Coastal Wetlands Planning, Protection and Restoration Act* (CWPPRA),[88] better known as the Breaux Act, the corporate giant took advantage of its environmental reputation and the federal government's heightened concern for endangered wetlands. In 1992, LL&E offered the State of Louisiana a cost-free, twenty-five-year lease that encompassed three of the State's western barrier islands – Raccoon, Whiskey and Wine islands.

Following the utter devastation of the barrier islands and the coastline caused by Hurricane Andrew in 1992, LL&E decided to make its agreement with the State of Louisiana an outright donation. Ravaged by Hurricane Andrew, the surface area of the three islands totaled little more than 1,600 acres. The final arrangement left the State with control of surface acreage.

Remaining true to its character and past practices, LL&E insisted only that the company retain all subsurface mineral rights. The federal government, the State of Louisiana, and LL&E, though, were not alone in this renewed interest in Terrebonne Parish's barrier islands.

James Voisin was leafing through reams of 19th century legal documents in the Terrebonne Parish Courthouse in Houma. The forty-three-year-old oil field worker had but a single thought in mind – constructing the Voisin family tree. For hours, Voisin had been scanning assorted legal documents when suddenly he fixed on a weathered brown pocket folder titled *Jean Joseph Voisin versus James Wafford, et al.*

Voisin emptied the folder and spread the contents on a nearby table. Midway through his review of the contents, Voisin eyed a yellowed 19th Century document. He stared at a passage copied from an even older document – an 18th century Spanish decree.

"A Juan Voisin, una pequena isla vulgaramente llamada L'Isle Longue…"

An English translation followed the Spanish entry.

"To Jean Voisin, a small island commonly called Long Island…"

As Voisin studied the pages, his mind drifted back in time to a story his father had once shared. During the 1950s and 1960s, Everett Voisin, James' father, operated crew boats throughout the Atchafalaya River basin for the Texas Gas Transmission Corporation. James Voisin recalled that his father once told him of a time when a company official related an interesting story. In the most casual of exchanges, the pipeline official told Voisin that he had once seen the name *"Voisin"* on one of the company's many offshore drilling maps. It was a penciled annotation

---

[87] LL&E, as the largest owner of environmentally sensitive wetlands in the continental United States, had a reputation of protecting its coast areas. For example, they instructed lease operators to take actions, such as burying pipelines (in order to not disturb the marsh grasses or fish and wildlife), promoting operations that prevented or slowed the rate of erosion and saltwater intrusion into the marshes. In 1989, the company was recognized by the Department of the Interior for its conservation efforts.

[88] *Coastal Wetlands Planning, Protection and Restoration Act (1990),* Title III, Public Law 101-646; 16 USC 3951-3956.

placed next to one of the small islands in the company's Trinity Field, an exploration area situated in the middle of the Isles Dernieres archipelago.

Everett Voisin then shared with his son James a story that had been passed down in the family for generations. It was the story of Isle Longue – now known as Last Island. It was the story of how the island had been illegally taken from the family - "*stolen*" by powerful interests more than one hundred years earlier. While the 1960 comment struck a familiar chord with Everett Voisin, in his mind, it did not warrant any action on his part. Too much time had elapsed and the cost of establishing ownership of a rapidly disappearing island would likely prove prohibitive.

Twenty-five years later, though, when James Voisin stumbled across courthouse records that documented his ancestors' unsuccessful efforts to reclaim the island, his father's words returned, wafting through his mind. It was a memory accompanied by two questions. What had become of Isle Longue and had the island really been stolen?

James Voisin shared his discovery with other family members. After some discussion, they decided to look into the matter. In the summer of 1988, James Voisin and his cousin, William R. (Billy) Boone, who was living in Kentucky at the time, retained the services of a Lexington attorney. Tim Hatton studied the documents the Voisins had assembled and then, on behalf of the family wrote to the Bureau of Land Management (BLM).

The Bureau, which had replaced the General Land Office in 1946, was the Federal agency responsible for the Nation's public lands. Hatton argued that since the General Land Office had overseen all 19th century public land transactions, its successor – the BLM - seemed to be the logical starting point. The attorney's request was low-key and matter of fact.

"*I have been retained by the Voisin family to assist them in locating lands patented to their ancestor, Jean Voisin.*"

"*The facts as we know them are as follows: Jean Voisin received an order of survey to Last Island from the government of Spain in 1788. In 1833, he applied to the U. S. Government for a patent to his property, pursuant to a statute passed by Congress in 1832. For some reason, a dispute arose over ownership of Last Island and the property may have been patented to others. I would appreciate any information that your office may have concerning severance of Last Island, Louisiana from the public domain...*" [89]

Hatton simply wanted official acknowledgment that the Voisins were the rightful owners of Louisiana's westernmost barrier islands. His letter to BLM included copies of two historical documents - a translated transcript of a 1788 Spanish *Order of Survey* and the 1835 Act of Congress that confirmed Jean Joseph Voisin's claim.

The inquiry languished in the BLM bureaucracy for months before being forwarded to the Bureau's Eastern States Office in Springfield, Virginia. Eastern States, the division within the BLM that has jurisdiction over public land issues in Louisiana, carefully studied Hatton's letter.

---

[89] *Private Land Claim of Jean Voisin*, Bureau of Land Management, Eastern States Division, Springfield VA.

A researcher with the agency responded to Hatton on February 21, 1990.

"This responds to your request [July 20, 1988] regarding a land patent for Jean Voisin, for land described as Townships 23 and 24 South, Range 15 East, Last Island, Louisiana."

"The records on file in this office, the National Archives and Louisiana Department of Natural Resources, indicate that T. 24 S., R. 15., Southeast District, State of Louisiana, was encompassed by the private land claim of Jean Voisin, confirmed by Section 1, Act of March 3, 1835 (4 Stat. 779, 780) entitled 'An Act for the final adjustment of the claim to land in the southeastern district of Louisiana.' Reference was also found in 6 American State Papers 665, 666, 667, 673, and 702, Gales and Seaton Edition (1834) under Certificate No. 50." [90]

The Voisins' attorney was ecstatic. The Bureau of Land Management acknowledged both the location of Isle Longue and the fact that the United States Congress had confirmed the family's old 19th century land claim. Hatton, however, noted that the BLM response inserted a troubling after-thought.

"Records obtained from the Federal Records Center failed to disclose the patent certificate referred to above. Please be advised, the fact that patents were not issued does not affect the title of said lands. This Bureau has no jurisdiction over lands after they have been patented and/or confirmed; title thereto vests in the patentee. Thereafter, the lands become privately owned and subject to the laws of the State..." [91]

The Voisins had received the official acknowledgement they were seeking or had they? Was the family's glass half full or half empty? On one hand, the Bureau of Land Management confirmed the Voisins' claim to Isle Longue. On the other hand, the family was sent packing back to the State of Louisiana. The jurisdictional adventures the Voisins were to face at home would consume the next five years. The journey in their state took them from agency to agency, courthouse to courthouse, lawyer to lawyer and politician to politician.

Finally, in 1995, the Voisins had come full circle. They were back where they had started in 1988, back at the door of the BLM's Eastern States Division in Springfield, Virginia. The family was ready to renew its questions of the Bureau. The real question, though, was whether *"full circle"* had taken the Voisins back to 1988 or 1849.

Chapter Nine: Had the BLM Found its "Honest Man?"

"On one bright, clear day, Diogenes was walking up and down the marketplace,

---

[90] Ibid.

[91] Ibid.

holding a lighted lantern high in front of him and peering around as if searching for something. When people gaped and asked him what he was doing, he replied, 'I am looking for an honest man.'" - from *Diogenes*, Laertius & Hicks, 1925

When the Voisins first approached the Bureau of Land Management in 1988, the family had, at least on the surface, gotten what it was seeking – official confirmation that their land claim was valid. The BLM, of course, stopped short of issuing a formal title to Isle Longue and instead pointed the family back in the direction of agencies within the State of Louisiana.

The Bureau's 1990 stance wound up subjecting the Voisins to more than four years on the bureaucratic treadmill. Getting nowhere and growing weary of the Bayou State's delaying tactics, the family decided in 1995 to make another run at the Bureau of Land Management.

In a repeat of 1988, the Voisins began with a letter. This time the family was determined to be more assertive. They would press the Bureau's Eastern States Division for an infinitely more tangible outcome. This time they would demand that the federal government fulfill an obligation it had under an 1835 Act of Congress - issue a patent for Isle Longue.

Expecting that the Bureau would at least address their specific demands, the Voisins were understandably consternated and perplexed when they received a response from Eastern States Associate Director Gwen Mason on May 10, 1996. Sidestepping the family's demand, Mason matter-of-factly told them that the Bureau is *"unable to locate the claim of Jean Voisin."*

In making that pronouncement, the associate director had reversed the stance the Bureau had taken in 1990. Then, just as the BLM had done in its 1990 letter, Mason added yet another disconcerting afterthought – the Bureau *"did not believe it* [the Isle Longue claim] *covered Last Island."* [92]

The pattern was increasingly clear, the Bureau of Land Management was sidestepping the most fundamental of questions – if Isle Longue and Last Island were not adjacent to one another then where WAS it located? Twice in a six-year period, the Voisins had approached the Bureau of Land Management only to receive diametrically opposed answers. When pressed to explain the reversal, BLM officials chose vacillation and obfuscation.

Perhaps the federal land agency feared it was opening a door to some unwanted legal or political repercussions. Unsure of its next administrative step, the BLM decided to turn to its parent agency – the Department of the Interior (DOI) – for *"an opinion as to the Bureau's position on this matter."* [93]

Officials at the Department of the Interior studied the Bureau's request and then decided to turn it over to its legal branch – the Office of the Solicitor - for analysis and recommendations. The

---

[92] *Private Land Claim of Jean Voisin*, Bureau of Land Management, Eastern States Division, Springfield VA.

[93] *Private Land Claim of Jean Voisin*, files maintained by the Bureau of Land Management, Eastern States Division, Springfield VA.

DOI's legal branch is comprised of more than three hundred attorneys. Approximately one-half of the agency's solicitors are located in DOI headquarters in Washington DC, with the remaining numbers stationed in DOI field offices throughout the country. Soon, the BLM request was soon resting on the desk of a young staff attorney in Pittsburgh, Pennsylvania.

Department of the Interior Field Solicitor Janet Goodwin was asked to take on a multi-faceted task - review the relevant documents, identify key issues, conduct additional research and provide advice and counsel to the Bureau of Land Management's Eastern States office in Virginia. Goodwin also read between the lines of her assignment. There she detected and inferred, albeit unspoken, requirement - produce an opinion untainted by the BLM's prior decisions.

The Bureau of Land Management had spent the past seven years dancing around the Isle Longue question for nearly seven years. Now the federal land agency had itself a lawyer. Perhaps more importantly, the BLM had itself a professional who was trained and committed to following facts wherever they led. Goodwin, wasting little time in identifying the essence of the BLM's nettlesome puzzle.

"It seems to me that the issue of location is not a legal issue; the answer must come from research into historical documents and maps." [94]

In Solicitor Janet Goodwin, the Bureau of Land Management seemed to have found its *"honest man."* Ever-methodical and uncompromising, Goodwin tackled her new assignment with vigor. On November 3, 1997, after only a few months of fact-finding and analysis, she sent a preliminary report to the BLM's Eastern States Office. In reality, Goodwin's initial communiqué was less a status report than a request for more information.

Doggedly thorough, the DOI field solicitor asked the staff at Eastern States for copies of the *American State* papers that the BLM had cited in its September 26, 1996, letter. She then posed a series of critical and relevant questions.

"Was the Gulf Coast west of the mouth of the Mississippi, ever called 'Barrataria,' and were the waters off that coast ever called 'Lake Barrataria'?"

"Is there, or was there in the 1700s or 1800s, an island in this area of the Gulf, called Brush Island? If BLM maps do not answer the question, could someone check the Archives?"

"Does Book No. 4 Orders of Survey Years 1785 -1799, United States Land Office still exist and does BLM have it?"

"Is there, or was there in the 1700s or 1800s, an island in the inland Barrataria Bay, called Wine Island? If BLM maps do not answer the question, could someone go to the Archives?"

"What would be the BLM's answer to a question of why acreage was not returned in the official

---

[94] Ibid.

survey for all of Last Island?"

Noting that Louisiana's Surveyor General had told General Land Office Commissioner Butterfield in 1850 that the Voisin *"claim had not yet been surveyed, nor has any order for its location been issued by this office,"* Goodwin asked the BLM to explain the phrase - *"order for its location."* Goodwin then posed one final question, one that was, perhaps, less a question than a harbinger of things to come for the Bureau of Land Management.

"Has there been correspondence with [the] Congressman over this matter recently? If so, may I have copies?

On April 10, 1998, DOI Solicitor Janet Goodwin forwarded a second report to Eastern States Director W. Hord Tipton.

"Last summer [1997], *the Solicitor's Division of Land and Water Resources forwarded their file...on the matter to me for handling. I have studied the box of documents, researched the facts and law, and drafted a summary of the situation, which is enclosed with this memorandum, along with a summary of the evidence in the file."* [95]

Her grasp of the key historical facts tightening, Goodwin was prepared to present her preliminary insights to the Bureau of Land Management. She began with an assessment of the BLM's initial support for the Voisins' claim.

"In 1990, the BLM...sent a letter to the attorney for the heirs which confirmed that present-day Last Island includes the Voisin claim. My opinion of the heirs' story is that it is plausible, and they have some very strong documentary evidence to back it up. I reviewed probably the same records and maps which resulted in the 1990 [BLM] letter." [96]

While acknowledging the plausibility of the Voisins' position, Goodwin confessed the need for additional research.

"The bottom line on the factual part of this puzzle is that more research of records is needed, and I can't do it from Pittsburgh. Someone needs to spend several days or a week at the National Archives, if we want the real story. Whether those waters were ever called Barrataria, is probably a question that can be definitively answered; and if they were, the heirs' story is probably correct."

Goodwin then posed another set of questions. This time, her questions seemed to touch a nerve within the Bureau of Land Management.

"In 1996, Cadastral Survey [97] *gave its opinion that Last Island is too large to be the 'Long*

---

[95] Ibid.

[96] Ibid.

[97] Cadastral Survey is the component within the Bureau of Land Management that creates and maintains survey plats and surveyor field notes for the federal government. Surveys of public lands that were conducted in the 19th

Island' granted to Voisin...could Deputy Surveyor Connelly have erred when he surveyed Last Island in 1838?" [98]

The DOI Solicitor was careful to let the BLM know that she was not passing judgment on the federal government's survey arm.

"I have no opinion on Cadastral's position, being totally unqualified to second-guess surveyors."

The question, though - *"...could Deputy Surveyor Connelly have erred?"* – rippled uneasily through the corridors of the BLM's Eastern States Division in Springfield. Given the critical role the General Land Office surveys had played in the westward expansion of the 19th Century, the Bureau's icy reaction was both predictable and understandable. Thousands of public and private land transactions had relied on the accepted accuracy of the federal government's surveyors. Within the bowels of the BLM bureaucracy, these survey documents – the official survey plats and surveyor field notes - were sacrosanct.

Was it possible that some of the surveys were inaccurate? Mindful of bureaucratic sensitivities and a growing coolness at Eastern States, Goodwin reminded officials at the Springfield office of some well-established historical facts concerning many of the 19th century land surveys.

"It is a matter of history that many of the old Louisiana surveys were faulty. In fact, this particular survey was declared to be erroneous in 1848 by the Surveyor General of Louisiana." [99]

Goodwin was unflagging in her pursuit of the case's historical facts and an understanding of what was going on behind the scenes at Eastern States.

"I am not sure what the BLM's position is. There appears to be an internal disagreement between the surveyors and the General Land Office records staff."

Were Goodwin's questions and observations beginning to unnerve executives at the BLM's Eastern States office? Was the Bureau beginning to regret its decision to ask for an impartial DOI opinion? Goodwin returned time and time again to the one question the Bureau seemed to be dodging. If Isle Longue was not co-located with Last Island, as the BLM was now contending, where was it?

"It is admitted that Voisin got title to some island, somewhere, but BLM doesn't know where...It would help if Cadastral could point to where 'Long Island' might be."

In her next report to the Bureau, Goodwin confessed that if the historical puzzle was to be fully

---

century are today maintained and overseen by Cadastral Survey. Cadastral comes from the Latin term "cadastre," which refers to a registry of lands. Cadastral surveying is the process of determining land ownership and the boundaries for townships, ranges and sections for public and private lands.

[98] Ibid.

[99] Ibid.

resolved, there needed to be additional research. She proposed a solution to the BLM.

"I have found this historical puzzle to be fascinating and am willing to conduct additional research, but would need assistance from your staff and travel funds to go to the [National] Archives. Whether to spend resources on this case is obviously your decision." [100]

Perhaps indicative of an uncertainty rippling through the corridors of the BLM, officials at Eastern States decided somewhat abruptly to terminate Janet Goodwin's assignment. The Bureau's decision was both curious and inexplicable. Ostensibly seeking an objective, neutral review of the Isle Longue question, the Bureau had turned to its parent agency, the Department of the Interior, for assistance. Field Solicitor Janet Goodwin spent almost two years following her analytical instincts. She was well on her way to connecting two hundred years of historical dots only to have the BLM precipitously withdraw its request.

In seeking the truth about Isle Longue, Goodwin had clearly unsettled the staff at Eastern States. Certainly, the Bureau's decision was unrelated to budgetary concerns. Travel from Pittsburgh to the District of Columbia to spend a few days poring over maps and documents at the National Archives and Records Administration (NARA) and the Library of Congress would have required only modest expenditures. In Goodwin's mind, this was all that stood between her and a final report on the Isle Longue matter. Something, though, within the Bureau had prompted their decision to end her involvement and return the file to Eastern States.

By the spring 1999, a weary Bureau of Land Management was ready to conclude its long, laborious effort to resolve the Isle Longue – Last Island dispute. After years of research, debate and analysis, the BLM crafted a final decision that was little more than a lukewarm, uninspired rehash of arguments put forward in the 1850s by those opposing the claim of Jean Joseph Voisin.

Eastern States Associate State Director Gwen Mason did little to mollify the concerns of the Voisins. By now, the family was convinced that it was not going to receive a fair and impartial hearing from the federal government. In her final letter to the Voisins, addressed to William R. (Billy) Boone – James Voisin's cousin – Associate Director Mason staked out the agency's final position.

"As you can see form the analysis presented above, the facts surrounding your claim, when considered separately and in their totality, do not support, in the opinion of the Bureau of Land Management's Eastern States Office, your assertion that the federal government erroneously transferred Voisin-family land to other private individuals and the State of Louisiana in the mid-1800s. In conclusion, the historical evidence does not support the thesis that Isle Longue…is the present-day (or even the 1850s) last Island."

"The information, in fact, tends to support the conclusion that Isle Longue was to the east of Last Island and situated in one of three large bodies of water called Lake Barrataria (i.e., Grand Lake Barrataria, Little Lake Barrataria, or Barrataria Bay), all of which were in the region of

---

[100] Ibid.

Louisiana that Spanish, French and early American settlers called Barrataria." [101]

Even in the act of closing out the Isle Longue matter, an ever-wavering Bureau of Land Management continued to hedge its bureaucratic bets. Mason ended her letter with a *"just in case"* observation.

"Further historic research may show that a Wine Island was located in one of those lakes. Even if one assumes that the 1788 Isle Longue was in the vicinity of present-day Last Island, it would be extremely difficult, if not impossible, to identify the specific present-day location of that 1788 island." [102]

Eleven years had passed and the Voisins were still without an answer to their two fundamental questions – *"where is our title to Isle Longue and if not co-located with Last Island, where IS Isle Longue?"*

Chapter Ten: History's Search for True North

---

[101] Ibid.
[102] Ibid.

"An error does not become truth by reason of multiplied propagation, nor does truth become error because nobody sees it." - Mahatma Gandhi

From the earliest days of recorded time, man's impulse to make sense of the world has turned his gaze skyward. Against the pitch-black canvass, ancient peoples studied the order and symmetry of distant twinkles and heavenly bodies. In that mystical darkness, they found gods and goddesses, heroes and villains, warriors and philosophers, animals and artifacts. Blanketed by an all-encompassing obscureness, they found direction.

Long ago, the ancients discovered that the imaginary line formed by the outer two stars of the constellation *Ursa Major* point unfailingly toward the northern hemisphere's brightest star - *Polaris*. Some call its location True North.

Why had the Bureau of Land Management, with all of its resources and history, failed to find True North? For reasons known only within the bureaucracy, the BLM decision-makers at Eastern States turned their eyes in a different direction and opted for a weakly disguised exit from the mess they called Isle Longue. Despite the fact that the agency spent considerable time and energy researching the matter, examining dozens of 19th century maps, poring over scores of obscure documents and studying its own internal records, it now wanted it all to be over.

One BLM researcher, alone, studied fifteen maps of the Louisiana coastline covering the 1804 – 1854 period and acknowledged that the coastal islands depicted on those maps were more often than not confusing in terms of names, shapes and location. [103] In explaining its decision to reject the Voisins' claim, the Bureau expended far more effort portraying an image of thoroughness and evenhandedness than being thorough and evenhanded.

In late 1997, sensing even then that the Bureau of Land Management was about to once again turn its back on their claim, the Voisins decided to seek support from two other corners – congress and the courts. The family's congressional efforts pointed first to Louisiana's two United States senators – John Breaux and Mary Landrieu. That overture was short-lived – a staff contact for each advised the Voisins that *"the senator is much too busy."* Undeterred, the Voisins turned immediately to their representative in the House of Representatives. Unlike his upper chamber colleagues, William Joseph *"Billy"* Tauzin II made time to listen.

A man of many talents, Louisiana's ten-term 3rd District Congressman was a master at relating to his constituents. Billy Tauzin, who hailed from the Bayou Boeuf town of Chackbay, just had an inherent knack for grassroots politics. A graduate of Nicholls State University and the Louisiana State University School of Law, Tauzin also had a well-deserved reputation for fighting entrenched interests, a trait the Voisins desperately needed.

In an effort to facilitate the ongoing discussions between the BLM and the Voisins, Tauzin instructed his Chief of Staff to serve function as liaison between the parties. Garrett Graves,

---

[103] *Private Land Claim of Jean Voisin*, Bureau of Land Management, Eastern States Division

Tauzin's eyes and ears in the proceedings, participated in several meetings between the Bureau and family representatives and never failed to remind the federal land agency of its repeated pledges to "*do the right thing.*"

It did not take long for Tauzin to realize that, when it comes to dealing with the Bureau of Land Management, a bit of gentle, well-placed prodding usually proves helpful. As it turned out, Billy Tauzin had just the right prod. The House Ways and Means Committee was in the middle of Fiscal Year 2001 appropriations and Billy Tauzin just happened to be the subcommittee chairman responsible for overseeing the budget for the Department of the Interior. Tauzin realized that the upcoming markup was his best opportunity to resolve the longstanding dispute.

The congressman realized that a successful resolution of the dispute would require at least a modicum of collaboration between House subcommittee staff and the Bureau of Land Management. In particular, Tauzin was not about to push for the expenditure of federal dollars until and unless he could secure from the BLM an acknowledgment that Isle Longue and Last Island were for all practical purposes one and the same island. Anticipating that the Bureau would support that effort, Tauzin used the DOI's Fiscal Year 2001 appropriations as the instrument to that end.

Tauzin inserted specific language and conditions into HR 4578 that were unambiguous. If the BLM formally acknowledged the historical claim of the Voisins, the United States Congress would recommend a final resolution to the matter – a resolution that most likely would include some unspecified level of monetary recompense.

"*The managers encourage the BLM to conduct a full investigation, including review of documents and evidence provided by the Voisin family to determine if the government transferred the ownership of Last Island, Louisiana while the property was owned by ancestors of the Voisin family. Should the BLM determine that the property was transferred inappropriately, the report shall include recommendations for the resolution of this issue.*"[104]

By the summer of 2000, however, it was too late. The Bureau of Land management had already made up its mind. They simply wanted an end to their historical ordeal. The Bureau's "*out*" was simple and direct.

"*It is the Voisin family's responsibility to find Isle Longue, not BLM's.*"[105]

Congressman Billy Tauzin and his subcommittee colleagues received that final response from the BLM in April 2001. To Tauzin's chagrin, the Bureau had simply parroted the stance it had taken in 1999. With their 2001 response to Tauzin, the Bureau of Land Management slammed shut the door on the opening offered by the Congressman's "*Intent of Congress*" language.

Having been burned before, the Voisins were not about to place all its hopes in one place. At the same time they working the halls of Congress, the family was resurrecting its legal options.

---

[104] *Intent of Congress* as expressed in *146 Congressional Record House 8472.64* (September 29, 2000).
[105] *Private Land Claim of Jean Voisin*, Bureau of Land Management, Eastern States Division, Springfield VA.

Determined to avoid the legal disappointments of the past, the Voisins were determined to return to court better prepared. To accomplish this objective, the family approached one of the Nation's most renowned scholars in the fields of constitutional law and land policy.

Hans Baade, a law professor at the University of Texas at Austin, School of Law, listened patiently and agreed to help. The Hugh Lamar Stone Chair Emeritus promised to review the historical facts and allegations surrounding the land dispute. He would then provide the Voisins with an analysis of the legal issues and his professional advice as how best to move forward in the legal arena.

On May 28, 1998, Baade conveyed to the Voisins and their attorneys his comprehensive assessment. He traced issues of sovereignty as control of Louisiana moved from Spain to France and then to the United States in 1803. Baade's treatise focused on how each territorial transition – including eventual statehood – influenced and shaped the management of the Louisiana's publicly and privately held lands.

Most importantly, Baade demonstrated how each change in territorial sovereignty affected the Voisins' historical claim to Isle Longue. The professor focused in particular on the status conveyed to Jean Joseph Voisin by the 1835 Act of Congress and how to apply that status to an effective legal strategy.

"The conclusion is inevitable that Jean Voisin had a claim to part of the then Spanish public domain of Spanish Louisiana by virtue of a regular order of survey issued by don Esteban [sic] Miro on October 3, 1788, which claim could have been, but was not, carried to title under Spanish law and custom in force at the appropriate time and place…"

"It is also beyond dispute that by virtue of an Act of Congress of March 3, 1835, Jean Voisin had an entitlement, as against the United States, to the lands described in that enactment by (indirect but unequivocal) reference to Class B Number 50 of the Register and Receiver dated September 5, 1833." [106]

Baade cited several precedents, each of which established the meaning of a *"confirmed"* land grant. Quoting United States Supreme Court Chief Justice John Marshall, the professor noted that while the United States may have gained sovereignty over the lands purchased from France in 1803, the 5th Amendment to the United States Constitution was nevertheless applicable. That amendment ensured that no person holing a valid land grant would be *"deprived of…property without due process of law."* Baade adduced that the Spanish land grants were *"governed by three basic rules."*

"First, they were vested property rights protected against encroachment by federal authority under the 1803 Treaty and the Fifth Amendment."

---

[106] *Voisin Family Papers.* Professor Hans Baade provided the Voisins with a large three-ring binder containing a twenty-eight-page analysis of the case, a summary of his reasoning and recommendations, and more than one hundred pages of legal citations.

63

"Secondly, as vested but as yet inchoate property rights, they were subject to verification and confirmation as provided by federal law."

"Thirdly, since post-1803 Louisiana was a so-called public land state (until 1812, a federal territory), and since the field was occupied by federal legislation, neither the extent nor the validity of these Spanish survey rights could be drawn into question by Louisiana law." [107]

Baade reminded the Voisins that even the Bureau of Land Management acknowledged that the General Land Office had never issued a patent for Isle Longue. He seized on what he viewed to be a critical point.

"Records obtained from the Federal Records Center failed to disclose the patent certificate for the Voisin claim, and it is my understanding that no patent therefore was issued to Jean Voisin or to his heirs. If so, it is hornbook law[108] that naked legal title to Jean Voisin's Spanish survey right as confirmed by the Act of March 3, 1835, is still in the United States, with the result that the jurisdiction of the Department of the Interior over the claim of the heirs of Jean Voisin continues..." [109]

The BLM's assertions notwithstanding, Hans Baade concluded that the facts in the case clearly established that the Isle Longue was, indeed, a matter that remains within the jurisdiction of the federal government.

"When, in 1835, Congress confirmed the claim of Jean Voisin by virtue of the 1788 order of survey, Jean Voisin became, in substance, the owner of the lands then confirmed to him. Nevertheless, since no patent was issued to him for those lands, naked title to them remained and (unless lost subsequently by the United States) still remains in the United States today. In particularly, it is the right and the duty of the United States to survey and to patent Jean Voisin's land right confirmed to him by statute in 1835, has survived the enactment of that statute." [110]

Baade did acknowledge that the issue of location regarding Isle Longue clouds the matter. While the original 1788 Spanish Order of Survey was *"patently ambiguous,"* with respect to location, Baade reminded the Voisins of the times.

"Such ambiguities could hardly be avoided when passing on orders of survey by a foreign sovereign couched in geographical references to largely uncharted and sparsely settled lands."

To the esteemed UT law professor, the essence of the case was clear and indisputable - the GLO and the BLM, its 20th Century successor, were legally obligated to survey all confirmed lands and issue a patent for each. Baade was adamant in his assertion that *"these procedures remain to*

---

[107] Ibid.

[108] *Hornbook Law* is a legal term that identifies a fundamental and well-accepted legal principle that does not require further explanation.

[109] *Voisin Family Papers* (Assessment by Professor Hans Baade).

[110] Ibid.

be pursued." [111]   At the heart of the dispute was the matter of due process.

"*It seems elementary that in the face of the Fifth Amendment, the United States could not, after March 3, 1835 purport to dispose of Jean Voisin's property without resorting to the power of eminent domain.*" [112]

Baade's report also addressed the role by the use of the 1849 *Swamp Lands Act*, which triggered a rash of land sales on Last Island between the years 1849 and 1852. In the judgment of the professor, the application of the *Swamp Lands Act* was wholly inappropriate. Quoting the Act, Baade noted that its provisions did not extend to "*lands claimed or held by individuals.*"   In other words, neither the federal government nor the State of Louisiana had the authority to dispose of a private claim previously confirmed by Congress.

The federal government, according to Baade, failed because it had never issued a title to land confirmed by Congress. This essential fact established that a required action had never been "*brought to conclusion.*" He further argued that it was the responsibility of the government – specifically, the General Land Office in the 1830s – to require the State Register "*to make out a full and perfect transcript of all the title papers and of the evidence in their office.*"

On April 25, 2005, the Voisins filed suit in the United States District Court of the Eastern District of Louisiana in New Orleans. Would this new filing – *James Voisin et al versus United States of America, et al* [113] – prove successful or lead the family down yet another dead end? Only time would tell and, as it turned out, the devastation left by Hurricane Katrina in 2005 gave the courts in New Orleans more than enough time.

On March 29, 2006, presiding District Court Judge Mary Ann Vial Lemmon's first ruling limited the scope of the case. Claims against the State of Louisiana were off the table. Acknowledging that this was, at its core, a claim against the federal government, she ordered the case transferred to the Court of Federal Claims in Washington DC. Lemmon's decision was unsuccessfully challenged by the Voisins' attorneys. Five months later, on August 18, 2006, the judge rendered her decision.

"*It is ordered that the Motion to Reconsider filed by the plaintiffs…is DENIED. The motion filed by the United States is DENIED…The motion filed by Louisiana Land and Exploration Company (LL&E) is GRANTED.*" [114]

Lemmon's 2006 decision, as well as a string of subsequent court decisions, made clear to the Voisins that their quest would continue to face one procedural or jurisdictional hurdle after another. Presiding officials never lacked for some technicality.

The case is not "*timely filed.*" According to the judge, Jean Joseph Voisin had been placed "*on

---

[111] Ibid.

[112] Ibid.

[113] *James Voisin, et al, Plaintiffs, v. United States, Defendant*, United States Court of Federal Claims, No. 07-54 L.

[114] Ibid.

notice" as of 1847 and, as a result, "*equitable tolling*" was not applicable.

The "*plaintiff's taking claim is time-barred...plaintiffs did not file suit within the applicable six-year statute of limitations.*

The Voisins "*slumbered on their rights and failed to file their claim within the six-year limitations period...[now] over 150 years later. Equity aids the vigilant, not those who slumber on their rights.*"

"*The court cannot toll the statute of limitations...on the ground that plaintiffs were waiting for the government to render a final decision and pay just compensation on the title claim for Last Island. The Voisins waited over 150 years before filing...*"

"*The Voisins have produced no evidence to suggest that the government concealed, or even attempted to conceal material facts...The Voisins were clearly on notice as to the government's actions.*" [115]

Each procedural ruling ended with the all-too-predictable outcome - "*case dismissed.*" [116] In the years following, Judge Lemmon's decision to dismiss, the Voisins continued to press forward on the legal front. Each effort and outcome turned out to be some variation of the ones that had come before. They specific reasons for years of failure may be many but the seed for those failures has been one – a complete misreading of the case's historical facts.

When Congressman Billy Tauzin asked the Bureau of Land Management to "*...to conduct a full investigation, including review of documents and evidence provided by the Voisin family to determine if the government transferred the ownership of Last Island, Louisiana while the property was owned by ancestors of the Voisin family...,*" he was acknowledging the critical role of history in resolving the one hundred and sixty-five year-old dispute.

Likewise, Professor Hans Baade understood the relationship of that history to the courts' willingness to rule on behalf of the Voisins' petition when he observed that "*if (and to the extent that) the heirs of Jean Voisin prevail in the location of Jean Voisin's land right today, they should also prevail in such [legal] proceedings.*"

So too did Janet Goodwin, perhaps more than any one person. The Department of the Interior field solicitor was leading the Bureau of Land Management toward an undeniable historical truth when the Bureau abruptly turned away from history. Was the BLM hoping to avert the truth about Isle Longue and Last Island? Historical truth, though, always has a way of surfacing.

In the case of Isle Longue and Last Island, the BLM was simply wrong. Had the agency stayed the course with Goodwin, it would have found that truth - a truth as unchanging as True North.

Chapter Eleven: For the BLM, Was the Past Prologue or Pretext?

---

[115] Ibid.

[116] Ibid.

"She that is queen of Tunis; she that dwells ten leagues beyond man's life; she that from Naples can have no note, unless the sun were post -- The man i' the moon's too slow -- till new-born chins be rough and razorable; she that -- from whom? We all were sea-swallow'd, though some cast again, and by that destiny to perform an act whereof what's past is prologue, what to come in yours and my discharge." - William Shakespeare, from *The Tempest* (1611)

From the outset, Department of the Interior Field Solicitor Janet Goodwin grasped the essential importance of getting the history right in order to resolve the dispute. Her focus on researching *"historical documents and maps"* was taking the Bureau of Land Management, though, down an historical path it did not want to go. Were Goodwin's unbiased eyes taking the Isle Longue research effort in a direction not to the liking of the federal land agency?

Did the BLM fear the additional research she requested would only serve to enhance the credibility of the Voisins' claim? Would Goodwin's review of another fifteen historical maps have actually uncovered an Isle Longue? If she found an Isle Longue on an old map, would it be in a location not to the liking of the BLM?

Was the Bureau fearful that Goodwin's efforts might cast a negative light on the historical reputation of the agency's survey arm – Cadastral Survey? Did the BLM fear Congressional intervention or legal repercussions? Were Goodwin's queries giving pause to the Bureau's decision-makers?

"What does the family want?'

"Is there a monetary amount?"

"How can you prove the documents presented are authentic?"

"What is the end gain if BLM can render a favorable view on your case, according to the evidence represented?"

"Could Deputy Surveyor Connelly have erred when he surveyed Last Island in 1838?"

"Has there been correspondence with [the] Congressman over this matter recently?" [117]

Historical truth seemed to make the Bureau of Land Management apprehensive and yet, in the end, the Bureau elected to use *"history"* as the cover for its eventual escape from the controversy. While such dichotomies always raise questions of motivation and speculation, there is a more pressing question – was the Bureau of Land Management right or wrong?

In fact, the BLM's reasoning was wrong. That conclusion is based on a careful reading of

---

[117] *Private Land Claim of Jean Voisin*, Bureau of Land Management, Eastern States Division, Springfield VA.

history. Administrators within the Bureau would have discovered that fact had they just stayed on the path Goodwin had set for them.

As for the Voisins, the family must have thought it was in a time warp. The last decade of the 20th century and the first decade of the 21st was an odd, incomprehensible replay of all that Jean Joseph Voisin had to endure in the lead up to the Civil War. The Isle Longue story is one of three distinct ten-year timeframes, each beginning in optimism, each ending with disillusionment and frustration in the 1840s, 1850s and 1990s, respectively.

In the end, the Bureau of Land Management made judgments that were at odds with historical facts and rigorous analytical thinking. The federal land agency based its final decision on four flawed conclusions – conclusions that were curiously framed and articulated in ways that suggested each of the four was based on unimpeachable historical research.

On the surface, each of the BLM's four reasons for rejecting the claim of the Voisins appeared thoughtful and sound. Each of the four seemed to have a basis in an exhaustive examination of dozens of historical maps, reams of documents, and the expenditure of countless staff hours. And yet, each is wrong.

The Voisins waited nearly ten years for the Bureau's decision. They received that decision in 1999. In its letter to the Voisins, the Bureau of Land Management spelled out its decision, point by point - four points.

1. Location and the Barataria Question

Opponents of the Voisins' position had long argued that if there was, indeed, an Isle Longue, it could only have been located miles to the east of Last Island. The 1788 Spanish *Order of Survey*, after all, describes an island located in Lake Barataria, some sixty miles to the east of Last Island. The BLM rejected the argument that at one time the coastal waters surrounding Last Island were considered a part of Lake Barataria. The Bureau's reasoning was unflinching.

"A French map labeled 1803 clearly places the region of 'Barataria' well to the east of present-day Last Island."

The unwavering conclusion of the decision-makers at Eastern States was clear - if Isle Longue was situated *"well to the east of present-day Last Island,"* then Isle Longue cannot be Last Island.

2. Isle Longue Was Too Small to have Been Last Island

Opponents of the Voisins' position consistently argued that the Isle Longue described in the 1788 *Order of Survey* and described in the 1835 Act that confirmed the grant was a *"small"* island, consisting of no more than 600 superficial arpents, or 507 acres.

The staff at Eastern States concluded that, given these descriptions, Isle Longue could not possibly be mistaken for the much larger Last Island, an island known to have been between twenty-two and twenty-five miles long and consisting of nearly 10,000 acres.

3. Reliance on a Questionable Map

During one of its meetings with Eastern States, the Voisins offered a copy of F. C. Laville's 1851 as proof that Isle Longue and Last Island were co-located. The BLM discredited the map because its originator – attorney F. C. Laville – was not a credible, impartial source. The attorney, after all, was an agent of Jean Joseph Voisin and it was his job to represent the interests of his client. The staff at Eastern States did not stop with simply questioning Laville's motives, they also argued that, other than the Laville map, there existed no cartographic evidence that an Isle Longue even existed.

"There is no island labeled 'Longue Island' on any of the maps other than Laville's map…"

By discrediting the Laville map, the Bureau effectively warded off any serious analysis of the land agency's official survey – the 1838 survey plat produced by G. F. Connelly. The BLM devoted considerable time and energy in the attacking the Laville map and defending its own internal surveys.

4. Occupation and Possession

The Bureau questioned whether Jean Joseph Voisin or his father had ever established a physical presence on Last Island. They leaned toward the oft-mentioned perception that Jean Joseph Voisin simply showed up on Last Island in 1848 or 1849 after learning of the island's growing popularity. The Bureau was curiously influenced by the fact Jean Joseph Voisin had TWO land claims confirmed by Congress in 1835. The BLM eagerly made the case that Jean Joseph Voisin could not have been in two places at one time?

"Both of the Voisin Claims No. 49 and 50 were based in part on continuous occupation and possession."

"Which of the two claims had continuous occupation?" [118]

The *"possession and occupation"* question enabled the BLM to cast a shadow over the motives of Jean Joseph Voisin. This issue was a not-so-subtle suggestion that Voisin was but a calculating opportunist.

In slamming the door shut on the Voisins in 1999, the Bureau of Land Management made clear to the Voisins that it had no plans to revisit the Isle Longue issue. The agency repeated that stance a year later when it turned its back on a solution proposed by the United States Congress.

---

[118] Ibid.

69

A new century was underway and the BLM simply wanted the dispute to disappear. To that end, the Bureau presented to the family its four reasons. In doing so, the Bureau was ignoring the thoughtful questions posed by DOI Field Solicitor Janet Goodwin, questions which, if answered, would have revealed the flaws in each of the Bureau's four arguments.

"Was the Gulf Coast west of the mouth of the Mississippi, ever called 'Barrataria,' and were the waters off that coast ever called 'Lake Barrataria'?"

"Were the waters off that coast ever called 'Lake Barataria?"

"Two of the three islands [Last Island and Wine Island] *named in the grant description are still called by their original names and show up on a present-day map in a cluster of islands: and that is very difficult to explain away."*

"What would be the BLM's answer to a question of why acreage was not returned in the official survey for all of Last Island?"

"I am not sure what the BLM's position is. There appears to be an internal disagreement between the surveyors and the General Land Office records staff."

"It is admitted that Voisin got title to some island, somewhere, but BLM doesn't know where…It would help if Cadastral could point to where 'Long Island' might be."

A careful analysis of the Bureau's four arguments is revealing. In ending the long, drawn-out dispute, the Bureau of Land Management simple reached back in time and cherry-picked four stale "*reasons*" to end the Isle Longue-last Island dispute once, and for all.

Why the BLM chose to end the dispute in the manner they did is unclear. It is also unimportant. What is important is that each of the Bureau of Land Management's four "*reasons*" was wrong but none of the four was as wrong as the first – "*Barataria Bay,*" the seductress in the Isle Longue story.

Chapter Twelve: The Subtle Seduction of Barataria Bay

"'First you will come to the Sirens who enchant all who come near them. If any one unwarily draws in too close and hears the singing of the Sirens, his wife and children will never welcome him home again, for they sit in a green field and warble him to death with the sweetness of their song...'" - Homer, The *Odyssey*, Book XII

"The singing of the Sirens..."

Nothing constrained the Bureau of Land Management's ability to reason quite like the impact of a single word - *Barataria*. Without ever realizing it, had the BLM had been *"warbled to death"* by the sweetness of one word? If so, how could that have happened?

For more than one hundred and sixty years, references to Barataria have dominated the Isle Longue-Last Island dispute. Its influence has colored the controversy with a dizzying array of constructs – *el Lago de Barataria*, Lake Barataria, Barataria Bay, Point Barataria, Grand Lake Barataria and Little Barataria.

Eastern States Associate Director Gwen Mason cited four reasons for rejecting the Voisins' claim but, in truth, one - *Barataria* - mattered more than the other three combined. From the outset, the Barataria argument has served as the lynchpin for the other three. Accept the Barataria rationale and the other three fall neatly into place, unquestioned and unchallenged.

Barataria was the first domino in a game that began long ago. Surprisingly, witnesses who testified during the 19th century legal proceedings were evenly divided, with each side offering impassioned and credible arguments for their respective positions. Those testifying on behalf of James Wafford viewed the references to Barataria as proof positive that Isle Longue could only have been located fifty or sixty miles to the east of Last Island.

Those supporting Jean Joseph Voisin, spoke in equally convincing terms about their belief that the term Barataria applied to a much larger body of water. These were, after all, men who had spent years sailing and fishing in Louisiana's coastal waters. They spoke with great confidence.

"The seaboard bordering on that part of Louisiana was...generally known by the name of Bay of Barataria or Lake Barataria...Isle Longue, and Timbalier Island were considered as being in Bay Barataria." [119]

"Yes, it was known as Barataria Bay or Lake as far back, as I can remember Isle Longue was in Lake Barataria. This coast was designated as Barataria. It has been called so, as long as I can remember." [120]

---

[119] Testimony of Jerome Moreno, *Public Land Claims, Number 4533*, National Archives and Records Administration.
[120] Testimony of Jean Pierre Cato, Ibid.

"I have heard it called Bay Barataria by Captain Allen, Pierre Tivet and Ganna [sic] and by others." [121]

With little or no explanation, the Bureau of Land Management casually discounted the words of experienced fishermen and pilots. Just as cavalierly, the Bureau adopted – nearly verbatim - the views of those who opposed the claim of Jean Joseph Voisin decades earlier. In its eagerness to adopt the unexamined views of those who opposed the Voisins in the 1850s suggests that the Bureau too had fallen prey to the seductive power of the word *Barataria*.

"[I have] never heard the waters around Last Island called Barataria Bay…and think such waters never could have been so designated without my knowing it." [122]

"I do not believe that the name of Barataria could have been given to these waters without my having heard it…I have now before me a map…on which Barataria Bay [or] Lac Barataria is laid down about four leagues east of Lafourche…[near] Grande Terre." [123]

"Barataria Bay is an inland bay some sixty-five miles east of the island claimed and is in the parish of Jefferson…Last Island is within the limits of the parish of Terrebonne [Parish]…" [124]

"Jean Voisin…asked Congress to perfect his title to a small island…which he describes as…being situated in Barataria Bay…a body of water as well known almost as the Mississippi River…" [125]

No one had been more instrumental than G. F. Connelly in framing the *"Lake Barataria"* argument. His repeated references to Barataria soon became the frame for the issue.

"Barataria Bay is a body of water as well known almost as the Mississippi River and has been so known ever since the earliest settlement of the country…with so clear and positive a description of the place where Voisin's claim should be located…[it was an] "impossibility that there should be any error."

"We are at a loss to imagine on what grounds he can pretend to change his location and move it to the parish of Terrebonne more than seventy miles west of the place described in the claim itself unless we should be uncharitable enough to suspect that the sudden rise in value of land on Last Island has excited his capacity to covet his neighbors' property." [126]

While Janet Goodwin's offer to continue her research efforts may have fallen on deaf ears, her efforts were able to coax the BLM into a grudging acknowledgment that the *"evidence does not definitively rule out the possibility that the waters around present-day Last Island were also*

[121] Testimony of Pierre Bromen, Ibid.

[122] Testimony of Adolphe Labauve, Ibid.

[123] Testimony of Former United States Congressman and Judge John Moore, Ibid.

[124] Letter from State Register Louis Palms and Receiver Henry W. Palfrey, Ibid.

[125] Statement of attorney Gilmore F. Connelly, Ibid.

[126] Ibid.

called Lake Barrataria."

The seductive nature of the word *Barataria* is altogether understandable. Both Goodwin and Eastern States archaeologist Jan Townsend spent months poring over dozens of 19th Century maps in the hopes of finding some hint that the waters off the Terrebonne Parish coastline had once been considered to be part of a larger Lake Barataria. Those efforts, though, were for naught. The Bureau's Eastern States decision-makers had already made their decision.

"Barataria is too far to the east."

The BLM was embarrassingly selective in its handling of the available research. Gwen Mason's 1999 letter to the Voisins, and the supporting documents, maps and internal discussions that led to that decision, were little more than a shameless regurgitation of the pro-Wafford testimony of the 1850s. Mason spelled out her conclusions with confidence.

"The information…tends to support the conclusion that Isle Longue was to the east of Last Island and situated in one of three large bodies of water called Lake Barrataria (i.e., Grand Lake Barrataria, Little Lake Barrataria, or Barrataria Bay), all of which were in the region of Louisiana that Spanish, French and early American settlers called Barrataria."

The Bureau of Land Management seized on its "*easy way out*" without ever answering the most fundamental question regarding Lake Barataria. It was a question Janet Goodwin had posited two years earlier.

"Was the Gulf Coast west of the mouth of the Mississippi, ever called 'Barrataria,' and were the waters off that coast ever called 'Lake Barrataria'?"

EVER called? Unknowingly, the Bureau in 1999 had fallen into the very trap that had ensnared the supporters of James Wafford in the 1850s. The BLM succumbed to the overpowering – and understandable - tendency to view references to *Barataria* through a 19th Century lens.

The BLM failed to grasp the very thing Goodwin was suggesting. The Barataria question is answerable and understood ONLY to the extent the issue is viewed through a contemporary lens – one that reveals the meaning of the word in a late 18th century setting. The flaw in the Bureau's reasoning is its 19th or 20th Century understanding of "*Barataria*" has absolutely no significance.

Like Goodwin, the Voisins had hoped to find an older map, one that showed that Lake Barataria covered a more expansive area along the coast. Their most promising find was a 1762 map by Tomás López de Vargas Machuca, which placed the "*L. Barataria*" legend in coastal waters adjacent to Grand Isle. The family cited three other maps - Mathew Carey's 1814 map of Louisiana, Charles Picquet's 1766 map and Thomas Bradford's 1835 map – all of which also displayed variations of the word "*Barataria*" in coastal waters just outside Grand Isle.

Of course on all of these maps, the legend *Barataria* appears east of Last Island. What then is the key to resolving the Lake Barataria piece of the Isle Longue puzzle? The answer to that question demands that the *"en el lago de Barataria"* be viewed in a 1788 setting. Do that, and the word *Barataria* takes on a different meaning.

In truth, the Bureau of Land Management's 19th and 20th century lenses revealed nothing about the contemporary meaning of *"el lago de Barataria."* No one – neither BLM researchers, Janet Goodwin nor the Voisins – ever uncovered an 18th Century map that placed the legend *"Lake Barataria"* in waters adjacent to Last Island. They failed for one obvious reason – no such map exists.

For some reason, the BLM never bothered to ask why no such map exists? The key to answering such a question hinges on one's understanding that the coastal waters surrounding Louisiana's westernmost barrier islands, including Last Island and Wine Island, were NEVER – or rarely – marked on 18th century maps of the Louisiana coastline.

In the decades leading up to the October 30, 1788 Spanish grant to Jean Voisin, maps of the Louisiana coastline typically identified only three coastal features: (1) the entrances to the Mississippi River, (2) the coastal waters adjacent to Grand isle and Grand Terre Island and (3) Cape du Nord (present day Point au Fer). The west, the next coastal annotation was Matagorda Bay, some three hundred miles to the west in Texas. Why were the waters to the west of Grand Isle not marked in the 18th century?

The answer to that question is embarrassingly simple. There was no need to do so. Settlers did not begin populating the Bayou Lafourche, Bayou Teche and Attakapas regions, in meaningful numbers, until the final years of the 18th Century. Areas west of the lower Mississippi River were, in the 1780s, sparsely settled. Because of this unquestioned fact, there was no need at that time to name the waterways, bays and islands west of the Mississippi River.

Historical maps of the Louisiana coastline mirror the evolution of the region. In 1788, the lands west of the Mississippi River were populated almost exclusively by an incongruous assortment of Native-American tribes, fishermen, hunters and trappers. Thomas Hutchins, in his 1784 description of the Louisiana coast, well understood this distinction.

"It is truly surprising, that the nations who have successively possessed Louisiana, never endeavored to obtain an exact knowledge of the sea coast westward of the mouths of the Mississippi. The many difficulties and dangers to which vessels are exposed in making, and getting over the shallow and shifting bars of that river, as well as in a long and tedious navigation upwards...to New Orleans, would render a harbour to the westward of the Balize, and a water communication with the upper parts of the Mississippi of vast importance...." [127]

This perception echoed an earlier observation by Antoine-Simon Le Page du Pratz in 1763, who described the four hundred-mile coastline from the Mississippi River to Texas as having but two named bodies of water - Ascension Bay and St. Bernard's Bay (present-day Matagorda Bay in Texas).

---

[127] In 1784, Thomas Hutchins published *An Historical Narrative and Topographical Description of Louisiana, and West Florida, Comprehending the River Mississippi with its principle branches...*

"Let us now resume the sequel of the Geographical Description of Louisiana. The coast is bounded to the west by St. Bernard's Bay, where M. de la Salle landed; into this bay a small river falls, and there are some others, which discharge their waters between this bay and Ascension Bay; the Planters seldom frequent that coast..." [128]

Annotations on Louisiana's historical maps, of course, began to change beginning with the first decade of the 19th Century. With the Louisiana Purchase in 1803 and statehood in 1812 serving as twin catalysts, settlers began pouring into the Lafourche and Attakapas regions.

Eighteenth Century maps consistently included legends for the passages into and out of the Mississippi River. The importance of the three passes is obvious. They served as the primary links between the Gulf Coast traffic and the vital waterway that connected the western edges of the United States. The only other marking for this part of the Louisiana coast was, as noted earlier, the frequently cited references to Lake Ascension or *Lac de Ascension*. Throughout the first two-thirds of the 18th century this legend was generally placed in the coastal waters fronting Grand Isle.

During this period, no other coastal Louisiana waters were reflected on maps. Toward the last third of the 18th century, the name Lake Ascension began giving way to *"Lake Barataria."* The single exception to this is that for a brief period in the 1780s, a few maps called these waters *Woods Bay*. [129]

An understanding of Louisiana's interior navigation routes for this period offers additional clues regarding the term *Barataria* and how that term was viewed in the 1780s. While the three passes of the Mississippi River served as the primary routes for larger vessels entering and leaving the river, there were a number of secondary routes used by smaller vessels. A network of bays, lakes, rivers and bayous permitted smaller vessels to travel from the lower Mississippi River through current-day Barataria Bay and the pass separating Grand Isle and Grand Terre Island.

One of these more direct interior routes would have been a logical choice for Jean Voisin when he sailed to and from Pointe á la Hache and Isle Longue. That, of course, raises the logical question - how would Jean Voisin have considered the term *"Lake Barataria?"*

Certainly, as Voisin passed between Grand Isle and Grand Terre, he would have considered himself to be in Lake Barataria. As he turned his vessel westward toward Isle Longue, would Jean Voisin have crossed some imaginary line signifying that he was leaving Lake Barataria? If so, where in the coastal waters to the west would that have been? When he *"left"* Lake Barataria into which body of water would he have entered? Logically, Voisin in 1788 would have

---

[128] *The History of Louisiana (Histoire de la Louisiane)*, by Le Page du Pratz (1763), page 216.

[129] A few late 18th century maps replaced the references to Lake Ascension with *"Ensenada de Palos"* or *"Bay of Loggs."* On other maps, this name was Woods Bay. *"Ensenada de Palos"* is Spanish for Inlet of Trees, suggesting that the entrance to interior waterways, primarily Bayou Lafourche was a heavily-wooded area. The appearance of this name on early Louisiana maps was short-lived.

described Isle Longue to Spanish officials as being "*en el lago de Barataria*," as opposed to some vague reference to "*unnamed waters.*"

There are other clues that support the contention that, during the 18th century, inhabitants of the region held the more expansive view of Lake Barataria. One map, an 1814 Mathew Carey map, places *Ascension Bay* in waters west of Timbalier Island and adjacent to Wine Island. The fact that Ascension Bay or *Lac de Ascension* appears on some maps closer to Grand Isle and on others closer to Wine Island suggests the more expansive view of these coastal waters.

A more detailed description of the coastline eventually evolved but only after settlers began populating the areas west of the Mississippi River in significant numbers. By the 1820s and 1830s, maps of Louisiana began identifying bays such as Timbalier, Pelto, Caillou, Atchafalaya and Vermillion because the region was more heavily populated and these western waters had greater significance. That explains why Wafford supporters and the BLM never understood the Barataria issue. They could only see the coastline in 19th century terms.

Goodwin had given the staff at Eastern States yet another clue when she noted the existence of a second 1788 *Order of Survey*. In March of that year, Governor Estevan Miro issued an *Order of Survey* to a man named Juan Chapa for "*a small island commonly called Brush Island, situate in the Lake of Barataria.*" [130] One Goodwin clue remains – a clue that should have reversed the selective thinking of the BLM. This clue is this - the 1788 *Order of Survey* placed THREE islands "*en el lago de Barataria*" – four, if the *Order of Survey* for Brush Island is included.

The glaring flaw in the BLM's reasoning is that it readily moved Isle Longue miles to the east because that is where Barataria was but ignored the 1788 references to the three other islands - Last Island, Wine Island and Brush Island. All four of these islands were described in the 1788 Spanish documents as being situated "*en el lago de Barataria.*" The Bureau chose to move only one – Isle Longue – to the east, ignoring the location of the other three – Last Island, Wine Island and Brush Island.

Janet Goodwin had given the BLM the answer when she observed that the Bureau could not easily "*explain away*" Wine Island. In many ways, Wine Island was True North for Janet Goodwin. It, however, was clearly not that for the federal government's esteemed land agency. The BLM's decade-long stare into the star-filled darkness revealed little more than the distant singing of the Sirens.

According to the *Enyclopaedia Brittanica*, the word *Barataria* comes from the Spanish word *barator* – a word that connotes "*to deceive or circumvent.*" A coincidence? Perhaps.

Whether the Bureau of Land Management was aware of the origin of the word is, of course, debatable. What is not debatable is that the BLM's use of the word *Barataria* certainly matched its inherent meaning.

---

[130] The French word for Brush is *Brosse*, which was the name indicated in the *Order of Survey*. Brush Island is situated a short distance from Timbalier Island, along the Terrebonne Parish coastline.

76

Chapter Thirteen: Size - Is a "Small Island" Really Small?

"On this small island, calm is surrounded by the loud rage of efforts to convince. I wonder why more people don't live here!" - Doug Minnis, from *A Small Island*

With its approach to "Barataria," the Bureau of Land Management left the clear impression that is was merely going through the motions. If there exists any doubt about that, the Bureau's second reason - *"Isle Longue was too small to be Last Island"* – dispels such a notion. As implausible as it may be, the BLM's approach to the *"too small"* argument was even less rigorous than its analysis of the Barataria issue. Once again, the BLM lazily reached back in time and plucked out a warmed-over rationale that fit an equally warmed-over narrative.

The Bureau's second reason has its genesis in a single phrase contained in 1835 Congressional Act that confirmed Voisin's original grant. In his recommendation for confirmation, Secretary of the Treasury Roger Taney noted that *"Jean Voisin claims another tract of land being a small island...called L'Isle Longue containing about six hundred superficial arpents."* Wafford's attorneys and their witnesses had seized on that reference during the 1850s.

"The area now known as Last Island is too big to be the small island described." [131]

"The land we are claiming is situated upon Last Island...and so far from being a small island [Last Island] is more than twenty miles long and containing about 10,000 acres." [132]

"[Last Island]...certainly...can be no 'small island' containing but 600 arpents!! The United States Surveys on file in this office show that the area exceeds eight thousand acres!" [133]

"The island described is supposed to contain 600 acres – Last Island is and was at the time Voisin's claim was confirmed, more than twenty miles long and contains nearly ten thousand acres." [134]

As they had done with respect to the Barataria issue, 19th century supporters of Jean Joseph Voisin offered a reasonable explanation.

"[Voisin] claims only what was granted by Governor Miro, the most western part...the part on which the ground is firm and solid, extending six miles more or less and containing according to his confirmation by the United States about six hundred superficial arpents." [135]

---

[131]   State Register Gideon Fitz, *Public Land Claims, Number 4533*, National Archives and Records Administration, Washington DC.

[132]   Letter to the State Register and Receiver signed by Pinckney C. Bethel, Thomas Maskell and Elias Beers, Ibid.

[133]   Response of State Register Louis Palms, Ibid.

[134]   Statement of attorney Gilmore F. Connelly, Ibid.

[135]   Statement of Voisin attorney, F. C. Laville, Ibid.

Just as Wafford's supporters parroted the "*too small*" argument, so too did those who testified on behalf of Jean Joseph Voisins. Jacques Terrebonne, for instance, reminded the court that the only "*high ground*" found was along a five or six miles stretch on the western end. Other witnesses for Voisin focused on that same fact - the western portion of the island contained only "*about six to seven miles of high and firm land, the balance of what was low and marshy ground.*" [136]

"*I cannot say how much firm and high land there was...the low lands were and are still covered by water at times...the high land principally laid at the point marked 'X' [on the map.*" [137]

"*The ground was high where Mr. Voisin had his house.*" [138]

As it had done with the Barataria question, the Bureau of Land Management cherry-picked its way through the "too small" testimony and simply inserted it into their 1999 narrative. When the BLM had completed that portion of its letter to the Voisins, it had an all-too-familiar ring.

"*All descriptions refer to...[IsleLongue] as being small. Some note that the island is about 600 superficial arpents, which is about 507 acres...The estimated area of the mid-1800s Last Island is about 6,000 to 8,000 acres. Given this amount of acreage, in no sense can one consider Last Island to have been 'small.'*"

The BLM's selective reasoning, of course, ignores the Voisins' argument that the "*600 superficial arpents*" merely pointed to the only habitable portion of the island - the "*firm and solid ground*" on the west end. The family's explanation certainly has merit. All parties to the dispute, including the BLM, acknowledge two facts about the island, as it existed in the antebellum period – it was more than twenty miles in length AND the only human activity ever documented was confined to the west end.

Several witnesses during the court proceedings of the 1850s testified that Jean Voisin and and his fishing partner Pierre Dinet operated their fishing enterprise in the area around the bayou and the "*firm and high*" ground on the west end of the island. As well, in 1819, explorers James Cathcart and John Landreth described the west end as the location of a fishing camp operated by Pierre Dinet. [139]

It is no coincidence that the 1848-1852 land sales – James Wafford, Thomas Maskell, Pinckney Bethel, Alexander Field, David Muggah, Elias Beers and others – were restricted to the six or seven miles on the "*high and firm*" west end. Did the BLM ever wonder why Last Island Village – the site of the popular summer resort – covered only the five or six miles stretch of beach on

---

[136] Testimony of Jerome Moreno, Ibid.

[137] Testimony of Pierre Bromen, Ibid.

[138] Testimony of Jean Pierre Catour, Ibid.

[139] In 1818, Secretary of War John C. Calhoun dispatched Cathcart and Landreth to Louisiana and Alabama to survey the coastal region for timber suitable for the building of warships. The two men spent nearly five months recording their observations. In late January 1819, the men spent three days on Last Island. The camp they described was approximately five miles from the western tip of the island.

the west end?

United States Coast Survey Assistant Ferdinand H. Gerdes provides perhaps the most credible insights into the make-up of the island. Gerdes spent weeks in the area in 1853, surveying and mapping Last Island and Ship Island Shoal. [140] The United States Coast Survey's map of Last Island, which Gerdes called *Isle Derniere*, focuses only on the western half of the island – a distance of about twelve miles from the western tip at Raccoon Point.

That Gerdes bothered to sketch only the western half of the island prompts an interesting question. What lay to the east? Gerdes' depiction of the island provides a clear answer. He described the area to the east of the hotel and bayou as the "*Duck Pond*" – an area that the renowned coast surveyor found to be low-lying, marshy and subject to frequent overflows.

"*Isle Derniere is an island of some twenty-two miles in longitudinal extent; on some places more, and on others less, than one mile wide. It is entirely level and low, with the small exception of a sand ridge, five or six feet high, running along the beach.*"

"*For eight miles it has been covered with thick chaparral; but during the last three or four years the western part has become cleared and thickly settled, and now becoming, during the summer season, a very suitable and fashionable watering place for the large population of the Attakapas and Plaquemines. There are at present, perhaps, sixty houses in the village of Isles Derniere, nearly all owned by planters.*" [141]

Ironically, the most compelling evidence in support of Voisin's "*high and firm*" explanation comes from the most unlikely of sources – James Wafford's attorney, Gilmore F. Connelly. During the court proceedings of the 1850s, Connelly seized on the "*Isle Longue is far too small*" at every turn.

"*The island described is supposed to contain 600 acres – Last Island is and was at the time Voisin's claim was confirmed, more than twenty miles long and contains nearly ten thousand acres.*" [142]

One hundred and fifty years later, Eastern States Associate Director Gwen Mason merely repeated Connelly's words.

"*Based on the evidence and standard usage of words and definitions, one must conclude that the legal description of 600 superficial arpents is an area that describes an island that is about 500 acres in size. In terms of size and shape, Last Island, as surveyed by Deputy Surveyor G. F.*"

---

[140] Ship Island Shoal, formerly Ship Island, was an underwater hazard to passing vessels. The Coast Survey meticulously charted its location and water depths in the area to aid pilots navigate safely along the Louisiana coastline. The Coast Survey also made recommendations regarding lighthouses lightboats (such as had been anchored at Ship Island Shoal.

[141] *Report of the Superintendent of the Coast Survey, Showing the Progress of the Survey During the Year 1853, Appendix 21 D*, Washington: Robert Armstrong, Public Printer (1854).

[142] Statement of attorney Gilmore F. Connelly, *Public Land Claims, Number 4533*, National Archives and Records Administration, Washington DC.

Connelly, does not fit the legal land description given in Jean Voisin's Class B, Private Land Claim No. 50." [143]

The BLM ignored the fact that Connelly's *"testimony"* was at odds with his own survey of the island, a survey he had completed more than fifteen years earlier. In November 1837, Deputy Surveyor G. F. Connelly surveyed the islands south of Terrebonne Parish. Last Island, because it was so long, required four survey plats. Procedures established by the Surveyor General's Office required state land offices to indicate acreage for those areas considered habitable. Reflecting the precise acreage for sections of a township was the way in which the State Land Office could identify tracts of land that were available for sale to the public.

In the case of Last Island, only one of Connelly's four survey plats returned acreage, only one of his four plats was formally classified by the Surveyor General as *"subject to private entry"* – the west end. The State Land Office indicated that that west end portion available for sale consisted only of 1,244.12 acres, not the ten thousand acres suggested by Connelly and other Wafford supporters in their court testimony. Once again, DOI Solicitor Janet Goodwin posed a question that the staff at Eastern States chose to ignore. The answer did not fit the BLM narrative.

"What would be the BLM's answer to a question of why acreage was not returned in the official survey for all of Last Island?"

Goodwin's question, of course, is relevant because it reinforces the fact that only six or seven miles on the west end were habitable. Every piece of evidence in the Isle Longue case makes that singular point. The *"high and firm"* west end argument is only part of the story. The real question is the origin of the *"600 superficial arpents"* entry in the 1835 Act of Confirmation.

The assumption seems to be that that that reference came from Jean Joseph Voisin. Was he, in fact, the originator? Did the reference to *"600 superficial arpents"* pertain to the actual size of Isle Longue or could it have another meaning? The Bureau, though, seems disinterested in answering such questions.

An understanding of the Nation's 19th century land policies places the *"600 superficial arpents"* reference in a different light. No one should have been more aware of those historical policies that historians and researchers in the Bureau of Land Management itself.

From the very beginning of the expansion westward, Congress placed limits on the size of land grants. Such limits also applied to the many pre-existing French and Spanish land grants. An 1804 Act of Congress, for example, restricted the size of the 18th Century Spanish and French land grants to one square mile. Similarly, when Congress passed the 1832 Act to *"finally adjust"* Louisiana's pre-existing grants, it added very specific language that limited the size of the confirmed grants.

"Provided, that no claim shall be therein recommended for confirmation, for more than the

---

[143] *Private Land Claim of Jean Voisin*, Bureau of Land Management, Eastern States Division

quantity contained in a league square." [144]

Of greater significance, and a fact that the Bureau certainly should have known, is that grants and transactions of six hundred acres or six hundred superficial arpents were quite commonplace throughout the 19th century. The Bureau's own historical records are replete with such references. Regis Bernody, for example, claimed a tract of land in the district east of the Pearl River in 1834. A subsequent court case noted that the tract *"contains no other description of the land granted than that it was 600 arpents in area, and was situated on the Mobile River, but that no survey of the land existed."* [145]

A review of the GLO's 19th century public land records reveals consistent and frequent references to grant sizes that were six hundred acres or arpents. [146] Examples include:

Joseph Vauchere *"recorded a land claim for 600 arpents on the River Homochitto"* in 1788.

John Hollaway recorded *"...a claim to 600 'superficial arpents of land' on middle fork bayou creek in Rapide County, Territory of Orleans"* in the 1810s.

"Certificates issued in possession of Dan H. Devaney. This was for 600 arpents in the District of St. Louis" in 1809 (*Land Claims in the Missouri Territory*).

John Patterson *"...received a grant or concession from Spain for 600 acres on the St. Ferdinand on 16 November 1802 based on a survey made for Juan Paterson in November 1798. His son, William Patterson, also received a grant from Spain for 600 acres based on a survey made in April of 1798"* (*Land Claims in the Missouri Territory*).

"Daniel Morgan Boone claimed 600 arpents of land in St. Charles, Missouri...1797."

"John Journey had Spanish Land Grant...600 arpents"...land on the Mobile River.

Joseph S. Murona was granted an *"area in arpens [sic] 600."*

"Christian Fender claiming 600 arpents of land, situated on Boise Bruile Bottom, Disgtrict of St. Genevieve...December 7, 1807."

James Flaugherty *"who came here in October 1799...received a Spanish grant for 600 arpents of*

---

[144] *"An Act for the final adjustment of the claims to land in the southeastern district of Louisiana, March 3, 1835 (4 Statute 779, 780)"* – from *American State Papers: Volume 6, Land Claims in Louisiana*

[145] Department of the Interior, Bureau of Land Management, Public Land Archives; History of the General Land Office.

[146] The three measures – acre, arpent and superficial arpent – are different but during the 19th Century were often used interchangeably. A superficial arpent (*arpent de Paris*) equals 0.84 acre. Superficial arpent and acre are measures of area. A linear arpent measures length or distance and equals approximately 58.47 meters.

land." [147]

Was it a coincidence that Jean Joseph Voisin described his island in such precise terms? Or is it more likely that the "*600 superficial arpents*" was suggested or specified by the State Land Office official who accepted Voisin's 1833 request for confirmation of his 1788 Spanish *Order of Survey*?

In addition, had Jean Joseph Voisin requested the entire island when he submitted his claim in 1833, his request would have exceeded limits specified in the 1832 Act – no claim of more than "*one square league*" was to be confirmed by Congress. Had Voisin petitioned for the entire island in 1833, he would have been asking for a grant that was twice the size as what Congress intended. One final observation is useful.

The original 1788 *Order of Survey* describes Isle Longue as being an island that is both "*long*" AND "*small.*" Could any description of Isle Longue - or Last Island, as it was known later - have been more accurate?

---

[147] Bureau of Land Management Archives

Chapter Fourteen: A Tale of Three Maps

"He had brought a large map representing the sea,
Without the least vestige of land:
And the crew were much pleased when they found it to be
A map they could all understand.
'What's the good of Mercator's North Poles and Equators,
Tropics, Zones, and Meridian Lines?'
So the Bellman would cry: and the crew would reply
'They are merely conventional signs!
Other maps are such shapes, with their islands and capes!
But we've got our brave Captain to thank
(So the crew would protest) that he's bought us the best – a
perfect and absolute blank!'"
        - Lewis Carroll, from *The Hunting of the Snark, Fit the Second* (1874)

From the beginning, maps have been at the heart of the Isle Longue-Last Island ownership dispute. Rarely have the central issues in the case – location, size, shape and name – been debated without reference to or reliance on one or more maps. Of the dozens of historical maps examined, two have dominated the discussion - Gilmore F. Connelly's 1838 survey [148] of Last Island and F. C. Laville's 1851 map of Isle Longue.

Perceived differences between these two maps were at the center of the legal proceedings of the 19th and, equally, at the heart of deliberations by the Bureau of Land Management in the 1990s. Where Connelly's map depicts a single island, Laville reveals two – Isle Longue and Last Island. Where Connelly's survey found no bayou on the island, Laville found a narrow bayou cutting through the west end, separating the land mass into two islands. The fact that these two maps were the creations of opposing counsel only encouraged bureaucrats to take sides.

Attorney F. C. Laville was Jean Joseph Voisin's initial choice to serve as lead counsel for the upcoming litigation. As the trial date approached, however, Laville concluded that he could better serve Voisin as a witness. Just before the trial commenced in 1853, Laville officially relinquished his position, turning lead counsel duties over to attorneys Charles Maurian, R. Miles

---

[148] Because Last Island is more than twenty miles in length and irregularly shaped, Connelly needed to produce four maps. The survey plat for the extreme west end of the island, which spans approximately seven miles, received the greatest scrutiny since it depicts the contested portion of the island. Original survey plats are maintained by the BLM in its Eastern States Office in Springfield, VA.

Taylor, and Miles Taylor.

In 1851, Laville travelled to the island to meet with Jean Joseph Voisin. The attorney spent weeks mapping Isle Longue and Last Island and annotating his map to reflect key landmarks, identifiers about which potential witnesses would testify. Voisin witness Pierre Bromen was one of several who pointed to the annotations during his testimony.

"I cannot say how much firm and high land there was…The low lands were and are still covered by water at times on the line marked on the plan from B and C, the high land principally laid at the point marked X…the balance of the island is all low. Last Island was a low marshy island…separated from Isle Longue by a bayou…" [149]

During his cross-examination of Laville and other witnesses, Connelly alternated his attacks between three primary issues – most of which dealt in one fashion or another with Laville's map. When Connelly was not discrediting his opponent's qualifications, he was questioning the motives behind the map.

Wafford supporters did not confine their attacks on the Laville map to the courtroom. In a letter to the State Land Office, Pinckney Bethel, Thomas Maskell, and Elias Beers pointed to what they viewed as significant differences between Laville's map and the State Land Office's official survey plat for Last Island.

"The diagram filed…is not correct as you can see by reference to the survey lately made by the surveying department of the United States…"

The final paragraph of their letter reveals an issue that has become central to the dispute - the contention that that Last Island and Isle Longue had undergone dramatic topographical changes in size and shape during the first half of the 19th century.

One of the keys to resolving the "topographical change" debate was the nature and extent of the bayou. Laville's map shows a bayou completely separating the two islands. Connelly's 1838 survey reveals no such separating waterway. During cross-examination, Laville calmly explained that the western portion of the bayou had dried up - *"disappeared"* - and, as a result, created *"only one island, of what had always been two distinct and separate islands."*

One hundred and forty-five years later, the Bureau of Land Management adopted verbatim Connelly's map narrative. In her 1999 letter to the Voisins, Gwen Mason of the BLM coolly dismissed the relevance and value of Laville's over-sized map.

"[The] apparent origin of the map significantly limits its usefulness in determining the true location of Isle Longue. Because this map was not prepared by an impartial third party who was disassociated from the case and the Voisin family, it is of little value in determining the true location of Isle Longue." [150]

---

[149] Testimony of Pierre Bromen, *Public Land Claims, Number 4533*, National Archives

[150] *Private Land Claim of Jean Voisin*, Bureau of Land Management, Eastern States Division

The Bureau's complete disregard of the Laville map did not apply equally to the Connelly map. This was a curious position for the BLM to take given the fact that both men served as his side's lead counsel and each created a piece of evidence that was central to his side's arguments. The BLM found a *"conflict of interest"* with respect to Laville but none with respect to Connelly.

On the surface, the two maps do seem to differ. And yet, when the Connelly and Laville maps are compared with a third, three amazingly similar pictures emerge. The third map in this cartographic trilogy is Ferdinand Gerdes' 1853 map of Last Island and Ship Island Shoal.

Gerdes, a pioneer with the United States Coast Survey, spent weeks in 1853, meticulously charting that portion of the Louisiana coastline. [151] When the Gerdes map is placed alongside the Laville and Connelly maps, two competing issues - the debate over the *"disappearing"* bayou and the question of whether there was one island or two - come into sharper focus.

What Laville calls *"Voisin's Bayou"* appears on the Gerdes map as *"Village Bayou."* The only difference between the Laville and Gerdes maps is the extent of the bayou. The Laville map shows the bayou fully encircling the small island. The bayou on the Gerdes' map follows a path that is identical to that depicted by Laville, suggests that the bayou had dried up a short distance from Raccoon Points, the location Laville's bayou reconnected with Caillou Bay.

On the surface, the Laville and Gerdes maps appear to be at odds with Connelly's 1838 survey. However, an understanding of a significant historical event brings the three together in a way that forms a singular topographical picture of Last Island and Isle Longue. What aligns the three maps is the *Racer's Storm* of 1837.

The powerful hurricane, so-named because the sixteen-gun British brig-sloop *HMS Racer* first spotted the storm in the Caribbean Sea on September 28, 1837, traveled more than two thousand miles. The hurricane wandered erratically across the south Texas and south Louisiana coastlines before turning inland and leaving a wide swath of destruction across Mississippi, Alabama and Georgia. The storm finally dissipated in the Carolinas.

Although little observable data exist with respect to the actual impact of the *Racer's Storm* as it passed over the Louisiana coastline, a number of newspapers reported its apparent strength. The National Oceanic and Atmospheric Administration, using those 19th century news reports, estimates that the storm would have reached Category Three status with winds topping out 115 miles per hour, accompanied by a storm surge of from six to nine feet.

Of greatest significance is the fact that the *Racer's Storm* passed over the Louisiana coastline and Last Island on an uncharacteristic west to east path that would have subjected the island to extraordinary forces from the south. The Category Three winds and the storm surge would have devastated the west end of the island.

---

[151] Assistant Ferdinand H. Gerdes was one of the most active members of the United States Coast Survey team. His most important works included numerous surveys of New York Harbor as well as detailed surveys of Florida, the Gulf Coast, and up the Mississippi River. His 1853 survey of Isle Derniere is unquestionably the most detailed and accurate map of the island.

The Bureau of Land Management was either unaware of the fact that a powerful storm had hit the island only weeks before Connelly produced his survey or the Bureau deliberately chose to ignore that fact. Acknowledging the storm, after all, would have complicated the BLM narrative. This information was certainly in the possession of the BLM. One of the documents maintained by the BLM is 19th century testimony by Voisin witness Pierre Bromen.

"Last Island was to the north of Isle Longue...[the bayou] was about two feet deep and in some parts, it was 6-8 feet deep. It was from 125 to 200 feet wide. I have passed through in on boats in 1837. This bayou on the west end...began to fill up...and I could not get through on my sailboat...It has been filled up by spents of sand and mud...caused by a heavy storm that occurred in 1837." [152]

Considering this and similar statements would have forced the BLM to reassess its judgments regarding Connelly's 1838 survey plat. Acknowledging the impact of the storm would have forced the BLM to reconsider its view that the island topography had changed little over the years. The Bureau would have had to consider that a storm of that magnitude and direction would have easily filled in the shallow, narrow bayou. Finally, the BLM would have had to consider that the force of the winds and the storm surge could have easily washed the low-lying portions of the west end into Caillou Bay.

The timing of the *Racer's Storm* explains why Connelly's 1838 survey plat depicts such a narrow west end. It also explains why Connelly found neither a bayou nor any signs of human habitation. Viewed side by side, the three maps validate the many reports and testimony about the west end's *"high and firm"* ridge, which, according to Connelly's survey, was the only portion of the west end to escape the ravages of the *Racer's Storm*.

Placed side by side (see page 86), the three maps serve as a reminder of Louisiana's changing coastline. Denying this reality is one reason the Isle Longue-Last Island dispute has persisted as long as it has. Conversely, understanding these natural phenomena is a key to making sense of the questions involving the bayou and the debate as to whether there was one island or two.

---

[152] Testimony of Pierre Bromen, *Public Land Claims, Number 4533*, National Archives

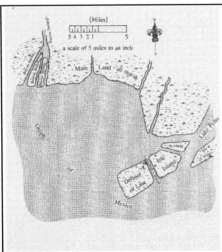

Those who remain unconvinced need only to turn to the 1819 journal entries of James Leander Cathcart and John Landreth, which describe *"fisherman's bayou."* In his journal, Cathcart uses a phrase that closely mirrors the representation presented on the Laville and Gerdes maps – a bayou that "[*makes] an island unto itself.*" [153] In addition, the Landreth journal includes a rough sketch (right) of the islands - a sketch that reveals three distinct and separate islands located just to the west of Wine Island.

Clearly, the notion that the topography of this narrow, low-lying archipelago never changed over the decades is simply wrong. The Bureau of Land Management, however, chose to ignore this reality and the facts.

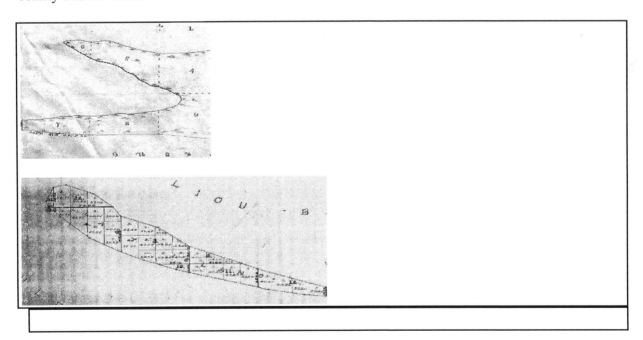

[153] *Journal of John Landreth, Surveyor: An Expedition to the Gulf Coast November 15, 1818 - May 19, 1819*, Milton B. Newton Jr., ed. (published 1985) and *Southern Louisiana and Southern Alabama in 1819: The Journal of James Leander Cathcart, Louisiana Historical Quarterly, XXVIII* (1945); Walter Pritchard et al., eds.,

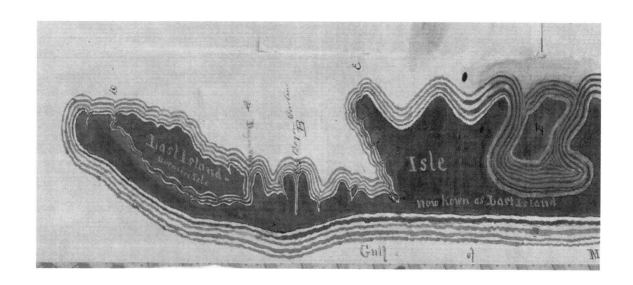

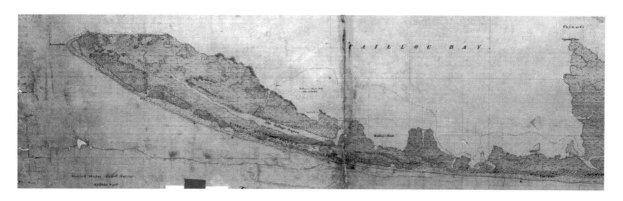

[Shown above are the 1838 Connelly survey plats for the western half of Last Island (top image), the 1851 Laville map (middle) and Gerdes' 1853 Coast Survey map (bottom). Each map depicts the west half of the island(s). The dashed boxes reflect the same approximate area (from Raccoon Point some nine or ten miles eastward). This is the location of the oft-mentioned "*high and firm*" ridge, which ran along the Gulf of Mexico. The three-map comparison, when viewed in light of the November 1837 *Racer's Storm*, explains much with respect to the "*disappearing bayou*" and the temporary submersion of the land mass just above the bayou – the small island Voisin identified as Last Island.]

Chapter Fifteen: Possession – Nine Points of the Law?

"A state of the law such as this, where possession apparently is not merely nine points of the law but all of them and self-help the ultimate authority, has little to commend it in legal logic or as a principle of order in the federal system."
- Robert H. Jackson, United States Supreme Court Justice, dissenting in
May v. Anderson, 345 U.S. 528, 539 (1953)

The Bureau of Land Management did not need a fourth reason to reject the claim of the Voisins. With their first three arguments, the Bureau had more than enough to make their stand. The BLM's final *"reason"* was, for the most part, a convenient afterthought, a bit of bureaucratic overkill.

In constructing its narrative, the BLM uncovered one final accusation used against Jean Joseph Voisin. Peripheral though it may have appeared, it was a perfect fit for Gwen Mason's exit strategy. During the court proceedings of the 1850s, there were periodic charges by supporters of James Wafford that Voisin arrived on Last Island only after becoming aware of the village's soaring popularity and value. What was the pro-Wafford story line? A simple one - Voisin wanted in on the action.

This caricature fueled what Connelly dubbed the *"continuous possession"* argument. Wafford's attorney insisted that no one – certainly not Jean Joseph Voisin – had ever inhabited or *"possessed"* Last Island prior to the initial 1848 land transactions. Connelly spelled out his position in a series of letters and depositions. In addition, while in court, Connelly made a point of pressing witnesses regarding their knowledge of people living or working on the island before 1848. He began with Adolph Labauve, who recalled the presence of but one person – Fifi Garcia.

"[Fifi Garcia]…lived in a small camp at the mouth of the bayou…[I have] no evidence of any [other] habitation on the island…"

Thomas Jones, another witness for Wafford - echoed Labauve's testimony.

"There were no inhabitants on Last Island when I first knew it. There was no indication to show that the island has ever been inhabited, excepting a pile of oyster shells…I know a man named Jean Voisin, now living on the island, have known him as a resident of Last Island for about 7 years." [154]

So too, did former United States Congressman John Moore.

"I have been on [Last Island] several times between the years 1834 and 1839 on fishing and hunting excursions… There was no settlement or vestige of settlement thereon in 1839. I found a [fishing] hut…[maintained] by Jose Matte, a fisherman for his own commission. I never heard of there being any settlement on it previous to 1839.…I first became acquainted with Jean Voisin when my testimony was taken before the Register and Receiver last winter…[I] never heard that

---

[154] Testimony from *Public Land Claims, Number 4533*, National Archives

any person of that name had ever inhabited Last Island previous to my first visit... I did not hear that the island was inhabited nor do I believe it." [155]

Wafford witness Mary Anne Scofield Beausergeant recalled only that the island had shown signs of the brisk fishing activity - *"One quarter of a mile from the Muggah Hotel, eastward was a fishery called Carlos' Camp."*

For every witness who denied a pre-1848 Voisin presence on the island, though, three witnesses offered an opposing view.

"[I was]...acquainted with Jean Voisin in 1802 on what was then known as Long Island, west of Wine Island, but is currently called Last Island..." - Jacques Terrebonne.

"I know an island called Isle Longue...became acquainted with it in 1811. I went there several times. It was three days at a time and I went out fishing with Mr. Dinet and Mr. Voisin, Sr.... I cannot say how many years [Voisin] lived there. He had built a wooden cabin and fixed up the things for his trade had a little patch where he raised some vegetables, and he was a fisherman, dried his redfish and sent turtles to market....I have known J. Voisin, Jr. from his early youth. In 1835, he lived at Pointe á la Hache..." – Jean Pierre Catour.

"I went there [to Isle Longue] to take permissions to Mr. Voisin, the father of the present defendant, who lived on the island. I was acquainted with Mr. Jean Voisin, the senior. He did reside on Isle Longue, I saw him there in 1812, 1813 and 1814. He was a fisherman, catching redfish and turtles. The redfish he dried and sent with the turtles to New Orleans. He had built himself a wooden house and fixed up the neighborhood for his fishing apparatus. He had also a small garden with vegetables, raised fowls and pigs.... – Jean Baptiste Benate.

Benate recalled that the elder Voiosin had a partner - Pierre Dinet – who *"...followed the same business as Voisin, they caught, dried redfish and caught turtles, for the New Orleans markets"*

"[I was]...acquainted with Jean Voisin on Long Island, now called Last Island, west of Wine Island, in 1812...." – Lange Lanata.

"I have visited it frequently in passing by on my way to the Sabine [River] and back, when I was trading in dry goods...This island... 'Isle a Voisin'... took its name from Mr. Voisin who lived on it....Voisin's home...was opposite the Bayou Voisin entrance" –Jerome Moreno. [156]

"I have frequently...visited this island...at least a thousand times for fishing, hunting and for the purpose of finding the channel...I know Mr. Voisin...he was frequently pointed out to me...I saw him but a few times...He built himself a pretty good house, known as Voisin's Camp and had all the fixings around it necessary for a fisherman. He was fishing, hunting and much a considerable quantity of them [was] to send to the New Orleans market..." – Pierre Bromen. [157]

---

[155] Ibid.

[156] Ibid.

[157] Ibid.

Bromen was also an acquaintance of the younger Voisin.

I know intimately [Jean Joseph Voisin]...*for the last 15 years in the parish of Plaquemines and on Isle Longue. He resides now on Isle Longue near his father's camp....for the last eight."* [158]

In order to counter the pro-Voisin witnesses, Connelly constructed a clever *"even if"* strategy. Even if the Voisins had been fishing the island for years, the family had not established a continuous possession of the island. The 1850s debate of whether Jean Joseph Voisin had actually lived on the island prior to 1848 was left unresolved. The great storm of August 1856 saw to that.

The *"continuous possession"* issue was simply a convenient add-on in Associate Director Gwen Mason's final letter to the Voisins. As if unconvinced of her own argument, Mason, inexplicably, decided to lift some language contained in the 1835 Act of Confirmation to make her case.

"Both of the Voisin Claims No. 49 and 50 were based in part on continuous occupation and possession...which of the two claims had continuous occupation?" [159]

Clearly, Mason had not bothered to read the précised wording used by the Act for claims B49 and B50. Had she done so, she would have realized that the two declarations were not at all contradictory. The Bureau of Land Management, however, was interested only in parroting the old pro-Wafford arguments. A careful reading of the two entries, which appear side by side in the 1835 Act, reveals their obvious differences. *[160]*

Land Claim B 49 – Voisin's claim for property in Plaquemines Parish (a small plantation located on the west bank of the Mississippi River near Pointe á la Hache) - was *"...claimed by virtue of ancient and undisputed possession, having been constantly and uninterruptedly inhabited and cultivated by claimant..."*

The claim for Isle Longue – **Land Claim B 50** – was *"...claimed in virtue of a regular order of survey...and of continued occupation and possession thereof ever since."*

The difference ignored by BLM is that one claim – B 49 – was based on *"inhabitation and cultivation"* of the property in Plaquemines Parish, while the other – B50 – was based on *"continued occupation and possession."* Why had the BLM not seen those differences? The Voisins lived in one place – Pointe á la Hache - and oversaw activities on the other – Isle Longue. The Bureau's misreading of the Act, conveniently allowed it to advance the theory that Voisin did not *"live"* on the island until 1848.

---

[158] Ibid.
[159] Private Land Claim of Jean Voisin, bureau of Land Management, Eastern States Division
[160] *"An Act for the final adjustment of the claims to land in the southeastern district of Louisiana, March 3, 1835 (4 Statute 779, 780)"* – from American State Papers: Volume 6, Land Claims in Louisiana

It is useful to point out that the language in the 1835 Act of Confirmation did not require Jean Joseph Voisin to live on Isle Longue. Indeed, the *"continued occupation and possession"* reference served only to indicate the basis of the confirmation. It was NOT a requirement regarding subsequent behavior. In fact, the reference to *"continued occupation and possession"* accurately describes the Voisins' historical connection to Isle Longue.

The evidence in this case, supports two conclusions: (1) until the late 1840s, the primary activity on Isle Longue was fishing, hunting or turtling and (2) there was a well-established and continuous *"fishing"* arrangement between the Voisins and the Dinets. Connelly, though, was determined to refute any notion that Isle Longue and Last Island were hotbeds for catching fish, turtles and oysters, The attorney for James Wafford missed few opportunities to suggest that the islands were too far west to have been a factor in the New Orleans fish markets.

"Was the fish trade of New Orleans very important at that time and were men in the habit of coming so far west as Last Island in order to supply...New Orleans with fish?" [161]

Just as Connelly ignored testimony that painted a much different picture of pre-1840s activities, the BLM ignored the widely circulated journals of Cathcart and Landreth. Those journals and several Voisin witnesses clearly establish a link between New Orleans and the island.

More importantly, that same courtroom testimony established an ongoing business relationship between the Dinets and Voisins, one that went back as far as the early 1800s. That connection was still evident during the litigation of the 1850s. In fact, Lucien Dinet was scheduled to testify on behalf of Jean Joseph Voisin during the summer of 1856. His appearance, though, like so many aspect of the case, was interrupted by the August 10th hurricane.

The fact that the Dinet-Voisin connection did exist, is reinforced by the frequent statements of Slidell attorney John Grymes, who often spoke of *"Jean Voisin and his business partner Pierre Dinet (de Nettei)..."* [162] The picture painted by Grymes regarding a connection between the Voisins and Dinets, is altogether consistent with the 1819 journal entries of Cathcart and Landreth. Cathcart mentioned Dinet in his journal entry dated January 31, 1819.

"A Mr. Peter Dunett [sic] of New Orleans, I am told has made a fortune by carrying on a fishery here. He always keeps three hands fishing and turtling and three carrying the fish and turtle to New Orleans market...." [163]

What are the facts regarding the Voisins? Clearly Jean Voisin and his son Jean Joseph lived at Pointe á la Hache (present-day Plaquemines Parish) until 1848 or 1849. Federal census reports show that for 1810, 1820 and 1830, Jean Voisin and his son Jean Joseph were living in Plaquemines Parish. It is not until 1850 that Voisin's name appears in census records living in Terrebonne Parish. These records are consistent with the view that Voisin moved his family

[161] Attorney G. F. Connelly, *Public Land Claims, Number 4533*, National Archives

[162] Ibid.

[163] *Southern Louisiana and Southern Alabama in 1819: The Journal of James Leander Cathcart, Louisiana Historical Quarterly, XXVIII* (1945); Walter Pritchard et al., eds.,

from Pointe á la Hache to Isle Longue in 1848 or 1849 only when it became clear that the State was selling off Voisin's island.

A reasonable conclusion is that Voisin realized that his only hope in forestalling the land sales required a full-time presence on the island. To think that Connelly and the Bureau of Land Management even had an issue with the *"occupied and possessed"* language is one of this case's curiosities. The wording of the two confirmed properties was, after all, quite precise. The B 49 language describes Jean Joseph Voisin as an *"inhabitant"* of property on the Mississippi River; B 50, on the other hand, simply says that Voisin *"occupied and possessed"* Isle Longue.

Somewhat comically, both Connelly and the Bureau ignore the fact that the owning multiple – and separate - tracts of land was a common occurrence in antebellum Louisiana. Indeed, most of the witnesses against Jean Joseph Voisin owned multiple properties. Certainly, this was the case with respect to former Congressman John Moore, Thomas Maskell, James Wafford and David Muggah. Speaker of the Louisiana House of Representatives W. W. Pugh was said to have owned all or a portion of more than a dozen plantations.

Did the Bureau ever question Congressman Moore's holdings? Did the BLM ever reflect on his plantations in St. Martinville and New Iberia – *Shadows on the Teche* – and wonder of the two locations - *"which had continuous occupation?"* Of course, they did not. Nor should they have. But the BLM did ask that question with respect to Jean Joseph Voisin. The decision to include the *"continued possession"* argument simply strengthens the belief that the Bureau was simply cherry picking its way out of the Isle Longue-Last Island controversy.

Another curious aspect of the *"continuous possession and occupation"* argument was Connelly's obsession with the date of the Louisiana Purchase. He repeatedly argued that the Voisins were required to document their possession of their island BEFORE the Louisiana territory passed into the hands of the United States.

"[The] affidavits may show possession and occupation as early as 1808 but any title in favor of Jean Voisin must necessarily have accrued prior to the year 1803…We further submit that parol testimony [164] cannot be received to vary the terms of a written title. But if such evidence be admissible, none other can have any effect than such as would go to show habitation and cultivation prior to the year 1803 and that the land inhabited and cultivated…vague statements as those made by the witnesses can have no effect whatever."

When Eastern States Associate Director Gwen Mason rejected the Voisins' claim in her 1999 letter, was she signaling the end to the family's protracted journey? Did future efforts hold for the family any promise, at all? Indeed, had the Voisins EVER had a chance to reclaim their island? To this last question, there are some answers – three answers.

Chapter Sixteen: Resolution – Three Bites at the Apple

---

[164] The word *"parol"* indicates oral testimony.

"It was the best of times, it was the worst of times, it was the age of wisdom, it was the age of foolishness, it was the epoch of belief, it was the epoch of incredulity, it was the season of Light, it was the season of Darkness, it was the spring of hope, it was the winter of despair, we had everything before us, we had nothing before us..." – Charles Dickens, A Tale of Two Cities (1859)

In deciding in 1999 to reject the Voisins' land claim, the Bureau of Land Management hoped to bring to an end a one hundred and fifty year-old dispute. It did not. After a brief interlude, the Voisin family resumed its legal fight against the establishment, turning from one court jurisdiction to the next.

Despite the family's outward appearance of resolve, the passage of time makes an eventual favorable outcome increasingly remote. The family, though, seems determined to push forward, seeking some semblance of resolution. Whether the Voisins achieve in the future some degree of resolution is, of course, questionable. What is beyond question, however, is that a favorable resolution had been well within their grasp – not just once but on three separate occasions.

The three instances share some interesting characteristics. Each spanned a ten-year period: 1835 through 1845; 1846 through 1856; and 1990 through 2000. In each of the three ten-year periods, the actions of a single individual were dominate, influencing events and preventing a resolution of the conflict. The degree to which the potential resolution would have favored the Voisins declined with each succeeding period. Each of the periods began with a sense of promise and optimism. Each, for the Voisins, ended in disappointment and disillusionment. The first of the three began with the year 1835.

Decade One: 1835 through 1845

For thirty-year-old Jean Joseph Voisin, the year 1835 should have represented *"the best of times."* The ten-year period, of course, did not end that way. Voisin's first great opportunity for a favorable resolution would fall victim to a decade of curious, costly inaction.

The chief architect of this lapse was none other than Jean Joseph Voisin, himself. His ten years of inaction and inattention sowed the seeds that would forever undermine the hopes of Voisin and generations of descendants for securing title to Isle Longue. There exists not a single indication that in the years immediately following Congress' confirmation of the 18th century land claim that Voisin ever requested title to or inquired about the status of Isle Longue.

This assessment does not mean that he did not make such inquiries, it means only that there exists no evidence of such an action, leaving historians and researchers to speculate. Perhaps Voisin assumed that following the Act of Confirmation in 1835, no further action was required. Perhaps he assumed that the State Register would automatically issue a patent for Isle Longue.

Had Voisin inquired about a title to Isle Longue shortly after confirmation, he likely would have been told that issuance of a patent would occur after the confirmed grants had been surveyed by the Louisiana Surveyor General. With respect to the survey of the islands along the Terrebonne Parish coastline, this took until early 1838.

Had Jean Joseph Voisin inquired about or requested title to Isle Longue during in the years following confirmation, he would have faced no opposition at all. During the last half of the 1830s, there was little awareness of or interest in Terrebonne Parish's barrier islands, other than that reflected by Jean Joseph Voisin's long established fishing and trapping enterprise.

Had Jean Joseph Voisin merely inquired during this time frame, there would have been no one to challenge his claim, no one to argue about the size of the claim, and no none to quibble about location or the meaning of the "*el lago de Barataria.*" There would have been no questions about a bayou and no debate as to whether Isle Longue and Last Island comprised two islands or one. Had Jean Joseph Voisin simply inquired, there would have been no one to stand in opposition. Spared such strident challenges and protests, the State Land Office would have simply issued to Voisin a patent for Isle Longue.

The "*whys*" explaining this decade of inaction and inattentiveness are intriguing. Jean Joseph Voisin petitioned Congress in 1833 for confirmation of two of his family's 18th century land holdings. Why did he obtain a title to the confirmed property at Pointe á la Hache but not to Isle Longue? Once again, the likely answer to this question is the *Racer's Storm* of November 1837.

All indications are that, throughout the first half of the 1830s, Jean Joseph Voisin and his partner Pierre Dinet maintained their fishing enterprise on the island. Given the immense power of the 1837 storm – a storm that struck only two months before the survey of the island - it is quite likely that Voisin chose not to rebuild his fishing structures on Isle Longue. Did he consider rebuilding and starting anew no longer worth the effort? While there may be other reasons, the timing of the *Racer's Storm* seems a logical explanation for Voisin's abrupt and unexpected detachment.

Whatever the reason, Voisin's absence became an open invitation to those who were destined to "*discover*" his island. The development of Last Island Village was fast-paced and frenzied and when Jean Joseph Voisin finally took notice, a new era was underway. As the year 1846 dawned, Voisin must have been reflecting on the words of Lord Byron.

"The thorns which I have reap'd are of the tree I planted; they have torn me, and I bleed. I should have known what fruit would spring from such a seed." [165]

Jean Joseph Voisin, however, was not merely reflecting on those words of Lord Byron, he was living them. Throughout these years of inaction and inattention, Voisin was "*planting*" the seeds of his own failure. The "*bleeding*" was about to begin.

Decade Two: 1846 through 1856

---

[165]   George Gordon, Lord Byron, from *Childe Harold's Pilgrimage* (1818)

In about 1846, people of power, position and influence began to discover the embryonic summer destination situated just off the Terrebonne Parish coastline. They had discovered "*Last Island*." The vacuum that Jean Joseph Voisin's inattention had created filled rapidly. Virtually overnight, the island metamorphosed into a wildly popular enclave for the wealthy.

Planters, merchants and politicians had found an escape from sweltering summer days. They delighted in long walks across the island's pristine white sand beaches. On Last Island, the Gulf winds were cool and fresh, life was slow-paced, idyllic.

Following the 1846-47 summer seasons, the steady stream of impromptu pleasure cruises began to give way to a growing interest in gaining a "*piece of the action*." Thomas Maskell had been the first to act. On April 8, 1848, the St. Mary Parish sugar planter purchased 160 acres on Last Island. Three months later, on July 13, James Wafford followed suit, purchasing a 53-acre tract. By the fall of 1848, Maskell was busily constructing a large two-story summer home on the Gulf side of the island, just to the east of the bayou.

When Jean Joseph Voisin learned of the sales and construction activity in late 1848 or early 1849, he immediately protested the encroachments by confronting both Maskell and Wafford with "*proof*" that he was the rightful owner of the island. Maskell and Wafford countered with their own certificates of ownership. Rebuffed and flustered, Voisin turned to the State Land Office and the man most responsible for blocking a favorable outcome for Jean Joseph Voisin - that man was Louisiana Surveyor General Robert W. Boyd.

Voisin's "*proof*" notwithstanding, Surveyor General Boyd shrugged and stated that his office had never surveyed an island called Isle Longue. In fact, he did not know where such an island was located. He was certain, though, that Isle Longue was not Last Island. For the Surveyor General, the issue was clear. His office had surveyed Last Island in 1838 and six years later, certified that certain portions of the island were available for "*private entry*."

Boyd's dismissive attitude toward Voisin was but a harbinger of things to come. On March 2, 1849, the United States Congress passed the *Swamp and Overflowed Land Grant Act*, [166] a law designed to encourage settlement of low-lying lands in the western states and territories, problematic The State Land Office promptly classified Last Island as "*swamp land*." With the *Swamp Land Act* providing bureaucratic cover, Boyd cavalierly commenced a land rush that would place the remaining acreage on the island's west end in private hands.

In the four-month period between July and October 1849, the State Land Office sold another 650 acres. Jean Joseph Voisin could do little more than watch as excited speculators gobbled up his island tract by tract. Sales on the island continued through 1852. By that point, the entire west end was in powerful, private hands. Not surprisingly, one pair of those hands belonged to Louisiana Governor Paul Octave Hebert. Joining the other buyers, Hebert quickly began constructing a magnificent two-story summer home on the beach.

Because land sales and the subsequent construction activity occurred at such a brisk pace, few

---

[166] The *Swamp and Overflowed Land Act* was passed by the United States Congress on March 2, 1849

historians acknowledge the brief opening for a mutually acceptable resolution to the Isle Longue-Last Island land dispute. One man – Louisiana Surveyor General Boyd – had the authority to simply suspend further sales activity until the dispute was resolved. Boyd was well aware of the conflicting land claims in late 1848 or early 1849. As late as March 1849, the dispute involved only three men – Jean Joseph Voisin, Thomas Maskell and James Wafford.

Challenged by only two men and with more than one thousand acres still under the control of the State Land Office, some form of resolution was still possible in early 1849. Boyd, though, chose to sell off the remaining tracts of land rather than resolve the dispute between Voisin, Wafford an Maskell. The decision by Boyd to continue the sales, soon left Voisin contending with not just two powerful, influential challengers but more than twenty.

Boyd's abrupt decision to sell off the rest of the west end left Voisin playing the weakest of hands. The case of *Wafford et la versus Voisin*, which was interrupted by the storm of 1856, did not hold the promise of a favorable outcome for Jean Joseph Voisin. Louisiana Surveyor General Robert Boyd had seen to that.

Decade Three: 1990 through 2000

The third chance for a favorable outcome presented itself to descendants of Jean Joseph Voisin during the final decade of the twentieth century Just as the other two decades began with a sense of promise, so too did the 1990s. Just as was the case in the two preceding periods, one person would turn the family's hopes upside down. That person was Bureau of Land Management Associate Director Gwen Mason.

When the Voisins first approached the Bureau of Land Management in 1990 to ascertain the status of their claim, the BLM was surprisingly accommodating. The Bureau's Eastern States Division responded in the affirmative.

"Records on file in this office, the National Archives and Louisiana Department of Natural Resources, indicate that [Last Island]…was encompassed by the private land claim of Jean Voisin, confirmed by Section 1, Act of March 3, 1835. Records obtained from the Federal Records Center failed to disclose the patent certificate referred to above. Please be advised, the fact that patents were not issued does not affect the title of said lands."

As would be its pattern for the next ten years, the Bureau's reassuring words reeked of indecision and ambivalence.

"This Bureau has no jurisdiction over lands after they have been patented and/or confirmed…Thereafter, the lands become…subject to the laws of the State."

The Bureau of Land Management had given the Voisins the two things they were seeking - acknowledgment of their lawful claim and confirmation that Isle Longue was, indeed, Last Island. The BLM's *"yes but not our problem"* stance sent the Voisins back to Louisiana, where they had started several years earlier. For four years, the Voisins trekked about south Louisiana, going from one state agency to the next, from one attorney to another and from legislator to legislator. Each new interaction became a hand-off to the next.

By the time the family returned to the BLM it was clear that the federal agency was hopelessly mired uncertainty and indecision. Looking for direction, the Bureau turned to Department of the Interior Field Solicitor Janet Goodwin. Goodwin, however, seemed to be taking BLM decision-makers in a direction they wanted not to go – support for the Voisins' arguments. By mid-decade, the Bureau was solidifying its "*yes, but*" posture. Yes, the Congress did confirm a claim to Isle Longue in 1835 but the BLM was simply "*unable to locate the claim of Jean Voisin*...[but] *did not believe it covered Last Island.*"

The family's one real chance for a favorable outcome rested on the efforts of Congressman Billy Tauzin in 1999. If Congress in 1835 could confirm their claim to Isle Longue, then perhaps Congress in 1999 could see the intent of the Act carried to its proper conclusion. At least that was the plan Tauzin had crafted. With a carefully crafted "*intent of the Congress*" paragraph inserted in the Department of the Interior's FY 2000 appropriations, the promise of an outcome favorable to the family seemed, once again, at hand.

Once again, though, a single person blocked any semblance of a favorable resolution. Tauzin's solution required but one thing – an acknowledgment by the Bureau of Land Management that the Voisins historical claim was a valid one. Eastern States Associate Director Gwen Mason, though, simply repeated what was now the Bureau's final position – no.

There is one remaining question. It is a question applicable to each of the three outcome scenarios. What shape would a favorable outcome have taken? There are three and each is different.

Chapter Seventeen: The Ever-shifting Face of Resolution

"And as I sat there, brooding on the old, unknown world, I thought of Gatsby's wonder when he first picked out Daisy's light at the end of his dock. He had come such a long way to this blue lawn, and his dream must have seemed so close he could hardly fail to grasp it. But what he did not know was that it was already behind him, somewhere in the vast obscurity beyond the city, where the dark fields of the republic rolled on under the night." - F. Scott Fitzgerald, from *The Great Gatsby*

The United States Congress confirmed Jean Joseph Voisin's claim to Isle Longue more than one hundred and seventy-five years ago and the matter remains unresolved still today. Identifying the eras during which a favorable outcome was within reach was relatively uncomplicated. Historical facts and timelines are indisputable. Equally uncomplicated was the task of determining in each of the three periods, the person most responsible for preventing a favorable outcome.

What is infinitely more difficult, though, is defining the shape of each of the hypothetical outcomes. While not definitive, there are some reasonable assumptions.

Resolution in the Decade of Curious, Costly Inaction (1835 – 1845)

Had Jean Joseph Voisin requested title to Isle Longue during the initial ten-year period, he would have found himself the beneficiary of not one but three possible outcomes. Which of the three depends wholly on two things – how certain provisions of the 1832 and 1835 Acts were applied and how those applications fit within the prevailing 19th century land grant practices of the federal government.

The first, and most important, of the two variables is the wording Congress used to establish the confirmation process. The 1835 Act confirmed the claim for Isle Longue that described an island of *"about 600 superficial arpents."* Based on this language, the Louisiana State Register could have simply issued a patent to Jean Joseph Voisin that consisted of six hundred superficial arpents, an acreage amount, coincidentally, that was commonplace during the first half of the 19th century.

The *"about"* qualifier contained in the Act, however, would have given the State Land Office some wiggle room. Given the absence of precise size, the State Register could have certified 600 superficial arpents or a larger tract of land, one that still fell within the limits of the enabling legislation. This is where the enabling 1832 legislation comes into play. The 1832 Act, which established the confirmation process, placed a limit on the size of the claims - Congress was to confirm no grant that *"exceed[ed] one square league."* [167]

Limiting the size of confirmed grants was commonplace during this era. In fact, the 1832 statutory limit was not at all unlike the limit prescribed in a similar Act of Congress in 1804. In that Act, Congress stipulated that 18th Century Spanish and French land grants were not to

---

[167] One square league equals 5,760 acres, or approximately one half of the island, as of the 1840s.

exceed "*one square mile*" or 640 acres. The "*about*" qualifier used in confirming Isle Longue in 1835 suggests that the State Land Office could have issued a title to Isle Longue for any amount of acreage from 600 superficial arpents to "*one square league.*"

Interestingly, there existed a third resolution scenario for this initial decade.   The State Register could have just given Jean Joseph Voisin a patent for the entire island. Given the fact that most of the island was low-lying, subject to chronic inundation and largely uninhabitable, the Register may have asked himself a very reasonable question - "*who would care?*"

From the perspective of Jean Joseph Voisin, any of these three patent scenarios would likely have been acceptable. By all indications, neither he nor his father ever utilized even five hundred acres in their fishing operation. They needed only sufficient acreage to accommodate several fishing sheds, a small house, areas for waste and oyster shells, their turtle pens and an area that gave them direct and convenient access to the bayou, which was critical to their operation.   Even a title to 600 superficial arpents would have met all of those requirements.

Furthermore, while Jean Joseph Voisin may have desired title to the entire island, he was in no position to make such a demand. A patent consisting of 600 superficial arpents, after all, was consistent with the confirming language of the Act.   The "*about*" phrase may have given the State Land Office some discretion but clearly the officials there retained the power to make the decision as long as they stayed within the "*six hundred superficial arpents*" and "*one square league*" ranges.

In contemplating this titling scenario, it is worth noting that at some point in the 1820s or early 1830s, the two islands – Isle Longue and Last Island – merged and became one. This is the likely explanation to the absence of any reference to Last Island in the 1835 Act of Confirmation. Unlike the original 1788 *Order of Survey*, which places Isle Longue between Last Island and Wine Island, the description in the 1835 Act simply stated that Isle Longue was adjacent to Wine Island.

Had Voisin requested title to Isle Longue in a timely manner – e.g., in 1836 or 1837 – neither the State Land Office nor Deputy Surveyor G. F. Connelly would have viewed Last Island as an uninhabited island. Connelly, instead, would have been surveying an island that had a pending request for a patent. Had Voisin requested a title in a more timely fashion, the connection between Isle Longue and Last Island would have been accepted from the outset. Had a timely request been made, the State Land Office would not have declared in 1844 that the west end was "*subject to private entry.*"

Jean Joseph Voisin, of course, made no such requests. Neither was he aware of the growing interest in his island. By 1846, steamboats and sailboats, filled with pleasure seekers, regularly made their way to Last Island's smooth white sands. The interest was so great that visitors were soon constructing modest cottages and cabins on the west end.   The Franklin *Planters' Banner*, in an 1847 article, noted island's meteoric metamorphosis.

"The steamboat Meteor No. 3, Captain Faussett, planned to leave Franklin Saturday, July 13 at 7:00 A. M. for Last Island offering a chance to the people to enjoy sea bathing and fishing, the

boat was to remain six days at the island...the Meteor could provide berths for 60 persons but was able to accommodate 80 without crowding. The houses on the island were able to accommodate 40."

Jean Joseph Voisin's decade of calm was about to give way to powerful forces.

Resolution in the Decade of Powerful Forces (1846 – 1856)

Louisiana Surveyor General Robert W. Boyd first learned of the Isle Longue-Last Island controversy in late 1848 or early 1849. Inexplicably, he chose to ignore the dispute between Voisin, Wafford and Maskell and continue selling off the entire west end of the island. This decision by Boyd eliminated any hope for a reasonable accommodation between the three men.

Before Boyd made this pivotal decision only three men - Jean Joseph Voisin, Thomas Maskell and James Wafford – had vested interests in the island. More significantly, prior to the July 1849 sales, only 213 acres had been sold, leaving more than one thousand acres on the west end still unencumbered. This critical point means that prior to July 1849, there remained ample maneuvering room for a negotiated settlement, one that all three men could live with.

Would Voisin have been receptive to such a solution? Two facts suggest an answer in the affirmative. Historical accounts indicate that neither Jean Joseph Voisin nor his father ever required or utilized more than a few hundred acres on the west end of the island. What was vital to their fishing and trapping operation, of course, was having acreage that abutted the bayou. Prior to July 1849, hundreds of acres adjacent to or astride the bayou remained available, more than enough to accommodate a house, fishing sheds, turtle pens, a boat landing, etc.

The fact that no such accommodation was ever proposed falls squarely at the feet of Surveyor General Boyd. He was in a position to use some portion of the remaining one thousand acres to satisfy both the needs of Voisin and the requirements of the 1835 Act. Instead of simply suspending further sales, instead of trying to clarifying the competing claims, instead of proposing a negotiated solution, Boyd opted to sell off the remaining acreage. He did so quickly and completely.

Had Boyd paused and sought to broker such an accommodation, would Voisin have accepted? For that matter, would Wafford and Maskell have accepted such a solution? Given the fact that Voisin never even used as much acreage as was confirmed in 1835 (i.e., the *"about 600 superficial arpents"*), acceptance of a negotiated solution would have been a wise and reasonable option. This would have left Wafford and Maskell with their 1848 titles and Voisin with acreage consistent with both his personal needs and the language in the 1835 Act of Confirmation.

Certainly the *"about 600 superficial arpents"* phrase would have given Boyd a significant bargaining chip. Interestingly, Wafford attorney G. F. Connelly even suggested such a solution in subsequent court proceedings in Houma.

"If Jean Voisin or his representatives are decided to have any right or claim on Last Island, such right cannot extend beyond six hundred acres,[168] *that at the date of the purchase by this respondent* [James Wafford], *there was a large amount of vacant land on said island – much more than necessary to satisfy the claims of said Voisin – and that said Voisin is bound to exhaust all the land existing as vacant land on the 18th of July 1848 before he can interrupt the purchase and possession of this respondent."* [169]

Boyd, though, elected to use the *Swamp Land Act* as his cover, thus throwing open the gates to the remaining acreage on the island's west end. By October 1849, more than a dozen new "*land owners*" had titles to land and each was busily developing his own slice of paradise. Boyd's curious decision quashed any hopes Voisin held for a favorable solution.

What motivated Boyd's actions is unclear. Clearly, he had the authority to suspend further sales until the dispute was resolved. Unlike the Bureau of Land Management, Boyd did not view the land office surveys to be sacrosanct. He often acknowledged that the early land surveys were fraught with errors and omissions. In his reports to Congress or to the General Land Office, Boyd often referred to his responsibilities to perfect the Nation's land records. [170]

"The incorrect and imperfect manner in which claims have been surveyed…and their incomplete connexion [sic] with the lines and corners of the public surveys, have been one of the most fruitful sources of difficulty which this office has encountered…it is towards the final settlement of these surveys that the efforts of this department should now principally be directed." [171]

Boyd understood and accepted his responsibilities. One oft-mentioned responsibility was the importance of correcting the flawed surveys of the past.

"Field notes returned, but not yet fully examined. Errors and omissions are known to exist, which will require correction…correction of old work found very defective…claims to be surveyed which have not yet been located."

Boyd specifically mentioned his office's role relative to "*surveys of private claims made under special orders of survey.*" [172] Had Boyd been influenced powerful interests? In the end, any chance of resolution of the dispute during this second ten-year period was all about the numbers. When the affected parties were three, resolution was readily attainable. Once the cast of characters exceeded twenty, negotiation and accommodation was virtually unattainable.

The Surveyor General, though, had slammed shut the door to a possible resolution, dramatically dashing the hopes of Jean Joseph Voisin for a favorable outcome. As the summer of 1856

---

[168] Connelly's reference to "acres" instead of "superficial arpents" reinforces the fact that the two terms were used interchangeably during this period.

[169] Statement of attorney Gilmore F. Connelly, *Public Land Claims, Number 4533*, National Archives

[170] *Report of the Commissioner, General Land Office, The Congressional Globe*, 31st Congress (December 12, 1849), pages 84 ff.

[171] Ibid.

[172] Ibid.

approached, it was clear that Voisin remaining hope rested solely with State District Court in Houma – and, given the powerful makeup the opposition, those prospects were none too bright.

Voisin faced some imposing forces in the courtroom as the summer of 1856 approached. Those forces, imposing though they may have been, were no match for the forces about to descend on Last Island. Dark, ominous clouds filled the horizon to the east. On August 10, 1856, a massive hurricane decimated Last Island and in the process ended eight years of legal wrangling over the question of ownership. The Great Storm directly or indirectly affected virtually everyone associated with the land dispute.

Those who did not die in the storm lost numerous family members and neighbors. A dark pall fell over South Louisiana, one that would last for years and then only yielding to an even greater storm – the Civil War. Ironically, the years following the 1856 hurricane probably afforded Jean Joseph Voisin one final opportunity to reclaim his island. In the lead up to the War, disputants on both sides, now in their fifties and sixties, cared little about ownership of a ravaged barrier island.

For the next 130 years, the unresolved land dispute would go unnoticed. When it resurfaced in 1988, the epicenter of the dispute and one last chance for resolution would shift 1,300 miles to the northeast and Washington DC.

Resolution in the Decade of Bureaucratic Ambivalence (1990 – 2000)

Throughout the 1990s, any hopes the descendants of Jean Joseph Voisin had for a favorable outcome, were at the mercy of the federal government. Clearly, the Bureau of Land Management held all the cards. Throughout the decade, the BLM repeatedly yanked the family first in one direction and then the other. The diminishing hopes of the family received a reprieve of sorts in 1999 from a most unexpected source - the United States House of Representatives.

During this decade of bureaucratic inertia, the Voisins had been anything but idle. While the Bureau was busy procrastinating, the family was busily working the halls of Congress. Rebuffed by Louisiana senators John Breaux and Mary Landrieu, the family received a much-appreciated helping hand from 3rd District Congressman Billy Tauzin.

The Nicholls State University graduate, no stranger to fighting powerful interests, was determined to end the Voisin's tortuous journey on a positive note. Tauzin had a proposal for the BLM, one that would afford the Bureau a safe escape from its self-imposed administrative quagmire. Tauzin proposed a solution that accommodated the interests of the Voisins without prejudicing the positions of the BLM or other parties to the dispute. The 3rd District Congressman and his staff inserted into the Fiscal Year 2001 Appropriations bill for the Department of the Interior language designed to end the matter once and for all.

"The managers encourage the BLM to conduct a full investigation, including review of documents and evidence provided by the Voisin family to determine if the government transferred the ownership of Last Island, Louisiana while the property was owned by ancestors

of the Voisin family. Should the BLM determine that the property was transferred inappropriately, the report shall include recommendations for the resolution of this issue." [173]

The BLM was asked only to acknowledge that Isle Longue and Last Island were co-located and, for all intents and purposes, one island. Tauzin also wanted the Bureau to reconfirm that the federal government had never issued a patent for Isle Longue. With little more than those two BLM acknowledgments, the Congress, working through the 2001 Appropriations Bill for the Department of the Interior, was prepared to do the rest.

Tauzin's proposal promised to end the controversy for all parties – the Bureau of Land Management, the courts, state agencies and, most importantly, descendants of Jean Joseph Voisin. The one barrier to such a resolution, though, remained the decision-makers at the BLM. By the year 2000, however, the Bureau of Land Management was firmly entrenched in its determination to end the Isle Longue-Last Island controversy. The Bureau's final response to the United States Congress was short and bittersweet.

"It is the Voisin family's responsibility to find Isle Longue, not BLM's." [174]

Congressman Billy Tauzin had reached across a 160-year-old divide and extended to the Bureau of Land Management an honorable way out of the dispute. Gwen Mason and her Eastern States staff, though, chose to spurn the Tauzin solution – a solution that would surely have shielded the BLM from the consequences of the General Land Office's 19th century oversight regarding Isle Longue. Tauzin had proposed a solution that would likely have assigned to the United States Congress the responsibility for dealing with any issues of compensation.

Instead, and after nearly ten years of prevarication, the Bureau of Land Management had extricated itself yet again and, in the process, closed off what was in all likelihood the Voisins' remaining hope for resolution. The Bureau must have viewed the end of the decade with a profound sense of closure. They had finally quashed a one hundred and sixty year-old land dispute. Finally, they must have thought – finally!

Had the Bureau of Land Management, though, learned nothing from history? Had it learned nothing from a dogged, determined family?

Chapter Eighteen: Lessons of the Labyrinth

"Socrates: Then it seemed like falling into a labyrinth: we thought we were

---

[173] *Intent of Congress* as expressed in *146 Congressional Record House 8472.64* (September 29, 2000).

[174] *Private Land Claim of Jean Voisin*, Bureau of Land Management, Eastern States Division

at the finish, but our way bent round and we found ourselves as it were back at the beginning..." - from Károly Kerényi's Dionysos (1976)

In his great philosophical work, *Dionysius*, Kerényi used words that Socrates might have spoken to describe the labyrinth in terms of a logical argument.

Socrates: *"Thus the present-day notion of a labyrinth as a place where one can lose [his] way must be set aside. It is a confusing path, hard to follow without a thread, but, provided [the traverser] is not devoured at the midpoint, it leads surely, despite twists and turns, back to the beginning."*[175]

Why had the Bureau of Land Management been incapable of resolving the one hundred and sixty-five year-old land dispute? For that matter, why were the federal government's premier land agencies – the BLM and its predecessor, the General Land Office – unable to even to locate Isle Longue? Had the Bureau simply grown weary, bewildered and confused? Had the agency just quit the search for a resolution?

For reasons known only within the Bureau of Land Management, the decision-makers were devoured at midpoint in the labyrinth by a bureaucratic fear of the truth. The BLM had turned its back on a plethora of clues and suggestions offered by its own researcher, DOI Field Solicitor Janet Goodwin, clues that would have led to the truth about Isle Longue and Last Island. Midway through, the Bureau simply quit.

Accusing the Bureau of Land Management of *"quitting"* is an admittedly harsh indictment. It is an indictment that goes not just to their actions and decisions but also to their motives. Such an indictment is doubly harsh given the Bureau's storied history and the role its predecessor - the General Land Office - played in managing the extraordinary expansion of the United States throughout the 19th century. The role the federal land agencies played in that expansion, and the role the BLM plays today in overseeing millions of acres of public land, has earned them a certain level of respect and credit.

It is in this historical context that the actions of the Bureau of Land Management seem so odd and inexplicable. The story of Isle Longue leads to certain inescapable observations about the role the Bureau played – observations and judgments that are at odds with its remarkable history.

Fairness and accuracy demand that the Bureau of Land Management be afforded an opportunity to respond to the accumulated evidence, inferences and conclusions that have emerged in the telling of this story. If the implication is that the BLM was interested less in the truth than in arriving at a just outcome, then the Bureau should have an opportunity to rebut such inferences. If the suggestion is that the Bureau was more intent on simply squelching the controversy than bringing it to a final resolution, then the federal land agency should have an opportunity to

---

[175] Károly Kerényi, *Dionysos : Urbild des unzerstörbaren Lebens* (1994), Volume 1. Working with Swiss psychologist Karl Jung and others, Kerényi devoted years to demonstrating a connection between Greek mythology and the study of psychology.

answer its critics.

In 2011, the BLM's Eastern States Division was afforded an opportunity to review the research, evidence and documents upon which this story's narrative and conclusions are based. The office that authored the 1999 denial letter to the descendants of Jean Joseph Voisin was extended the opportunity to offer any rebuttal they deemed appropriate. After one or two days of internal discussions – presumably with their in-house counsel – a spokesperson for the Eastern States Division of the BLM declined the offer.

"We appreciate the opportunity but will pass."

Thus, the story's overriding conclusion is that the BLM chose simply to walk away, without resolution, without answers, without really knowing the truth about Isle Longue and Last Island. Had the Bureau simply followed the breadcrumbs left by Solicitor Janet Goodwin, it would have arrived at answers that make sense. Instead the BLM quit at the midway point.

Had the BLM simply followed Goodwin's clues and suggestions, answered the questions she posed, it would have found their answers and some level of resolution for the Voisins. Had the Bureau pushed on, back to the beginning, it would have solved the riddle that was Barataria Bay.

Had it continued along the path suggested by Goodwin, the BLM would have understood that, in fact, the early land surveys were often flawed and fraught with errors – historical errors and omissions that would have made a reassessment of the facts a reasonable response. Had the BLM continued, it would have resolved the *"Isle Longue is too small to be Last Island"* perception.

Had it continued, the Bureau would have viewed the *"continuous possession"* differently. Had the Bureau of Land Management but pushed forward, they would have inevitably returned to the beginning and the answer to the Isle Longue question – an answer rooted in the 1788 Spanish Order of Survey. But for reasons known only to decision-makers within the BLM, they chose to quit a midpoint, unaware that the answer to the Isle Longue puzzle would have been found simply by returning to the beginning.

Labyrinths are like that.

Epilogue

"How do you pick up the threads of an old life? How do you go on, when in

106

your heart you begin to understand there is no going back. There are some things that time cannot mend. Some hurts that go too deep...that have taken hold." - J. R. R. Tolkien, from *Lord of the Rings* (1954)

Some called her the *"wandering widow of Last Island."* It seems an altogether fitting appellation. For more than one hundred and fifty years, some member of the Voisin family has followed a road that never was, a road that might one day be – a road that in reality was marked only by fleeting, vaporous hopes. So many times, the story of Isle Longue has seemingly come to its inevitable, merciful end, only to see a family's aspirations spring forth yet again.

For more than one hundred years, citizens of history-rich south Louisiana pause each October to remember those who had come before. In many south Louisiana communities, these annual remembrances include tours of antebellum plantation homes and cemeteries. Some communities call the event their annual *"Ghost Walk."* To some it is just a seasonal fest. To others it is a day of remembrance.

The St. Mary Parish town of Franklin, which straddles the meandering magnificence of Bayou Teche, is no exception to this somber tradition. Recently, Jeanette Voisin described her recent participation in the annual St. Mary Parish cemetery tour.

"I represented the Voisins. I paraded around the cemetery with some clothes from that time period. I was the wandering widow, wearing a long black dress with a black veil covering my face."

"I cried all day long."

There are, of course, some things – some people – destined to drift through the endless reach of time. Descendants of Jean Voisin have carried their struggle to reclaim Isle Longue into a third century.

James Voisin, great-great-great grandson of Jean Voisin, led the family's struggle for nearly twenty years. James Voisin died on January 8, 2009 – almost one year to the day from the 2008 Federal Court of Appeals decision to dismiss the case.

During memorial services for James Voisin, sixteen year-old Gage Rodriguez spoke eloquently about his grandfather, sharing the most intimate of stories with bereaved family members and friends. Before concluding his remarks, Gage paused for a final reflection and then quoted novelist John Steinbeck.

"The clock wound by Elizabeth still ticked, storing in its spring the presence of her hand, and the wool socks she had hung to dry were still damp. These were vital parts of Elizabeth that were not dead yet. Joseph pondered slowly over it - life cannot be cut off quickly. One cannot be dead until the things he changed are dead. His effect is the only evidence of his life. While there remains even a plaintive memory, a person cannot be cutoff, dead. And he thought, 'It's a long slow process for a human to die.... a man's life dies as a commotion in a still pool dies, in little

107

waves, spreading and growing back toward stillness. '" [176]

James Voisin was dead, his body at rest. Still alive, though, is the family's decades-long struggle to reclaim Isle Longue. It is a quest that has changed with time. The Voisins will continue to seek title to *"their island."* But they will do so in recognition of the fact that today *"their island"* is comprised of little more than four rapidly-shrinking spits of sand in the Gulf of Mexico. Most of what was once Last Island – Isle Longue – has given way to the open waters of the Gulf of Mexico.

For decades, the Voisins have sought some form of acknowledgement, some semblance of recompense, only to have their hopes dashed. The opening provided by Congressman Billy Tauzin and the United States House of Representatives in 2000 has virtually no chance of being revisited. The monetary solution contemplated in 2000 no longer exists in the era of trillion-dollar deficits.

Expecting the state or federal courts to resolve the matter is equally unlikely. One may dream that some supreme body will one day quantify who lost and who gained over the decades but stark reality suggests that such a result is highly unlikely. And so, the question - what remains to be gained by the family's struggle?

Sir Arthur Conan Doyle once observed: *"Once you eliminate the impossible, whatever remains, no matter how improbable, must be the truth."*

With each passing year, the likelihood of some tangible outcome favorable to the Voisins diminishes. In time, even the hopes of the most determined family evaporates. When that point is reached, only one thing will be left - the truth. It is a truth that persists as ripples on the open waters. It is a truth that remains as stored in a wound spring – a spring that commands the clock to continue ticking.

The truth about Isle Longue and Last Island still waits to be reclaimed. When that moment comes, some will smile with bemusement. They will smile because the truth about Isle Longue and Last Island will be found where it had been for more than two hundred and twenty years – where it has always been. The truth will be found because someone bothered to journey forth, bothered to follow a path that led back to the beginning.

"To Jean Voisin, a small island, commonly called L'Isle Longue, situated in the Lake of Barrataria, adjoining...on one side Last Island, and on the other, fronting the island called Wine Island."

- 30 –

---

[176] from *To a God Unknown* by John Steinbeck (1933)

Made in the USA
San Bernardino, CA
06 October 2015